WISDOM
OF THE
UNSHAKEABLE

UNLOCKING PEACE, RESILIENCE
AND TRANSFORMATION

By - Amritha Kailas

For more information, email samsarga.ca@gmail.com.
ISBN: 979-8-89109-250-1 - paperback
ISBN: 979-8-89109-251-8 - ebook

Dedication

Dedicated to the Almighty, all my teachers & coaches, my grandparents, mother, husband, and my beautiful girls who believed in me and supported me throughout my life's journey in making my dreams come true.

Table of Contents

INTRODUCTION

ARE YOU READY TO BEGIN the journey?

For generations, people in this world have gone through emotional suffering in their lives that has made them feel stuck, lonely, anxious, and disappointed. This emotional dissatisfaction has not only led to severe mental health issues but also to heartbreaks, loss of lives, family conflicts, wars, and enmity.

Based on a 2017 study published on Future Learn,[1] it is estimated that 792 million people live with a mental health disorder, translating to 10.7% of the global population. The most prevalent disorders were anxiety (284 million people, 3.8% of the population) and depression (264 million people, 3.4%).

To overcome this mental suffering and discover peace, we run after people, places, power, money, and other material things around us. I also ran a similar race.

I was born into a family where peace was a rare commodity, and domestic violence was a daily ritual. My assets were faith in God, perseverance, determination, and support from my mother, grandparents, teachers, and friends.

Every time I faced a hard blow, I asked God, "Why me?" I could not escape these problematic situations, and I had no choice but to face them. From the early age of three years old, I was blamed for the family conflicts. Every action that I performed was negatively criticized. I slowly began believing in the negative remarks, starting to think that I was not good enough and that something was wrong with me. Over the years, this self-doubt grew

---

1   Future Learn, "The State of Global Mental Health."

larger and shielded my true personality underneath. Every time I came across a negative situation or person, this self-doubt popped up with feelings of sorrow, worry, and anxiety, which obstructed me from expressing my authentic self and leading a life of peace and confidence. As I did not know the way to overcome it at that time, I just suppressed it into the deep corners of my mind for nobody to discover.

I was deeply attached to my grandfather who was highly spiritual and lived by solid principles and values in life. Because I was surrounded by talks on spirituality and was taken to the abodes of various great spiritual masters, I began relying on a higher power to work wonders in my life.

Years passed, and it was when I was ten years old that I was introduced to the holy text, the Bhagavad Gita, by my grandmother. She gave me the book and told me whenever I had a problem, I could open this book and find a solution. I had no clue what treasure was hidden within this holy text, but I blindly agreed. After a few months, my parents were transferred to a new location for their jobs, so I had to move to a new school. One of the requirements for admission into the school was to know the Sanskrit language. I had yet to learn this language before. So my parents decided to send me to a Sanskrit teacher during my summer break.

With just one month left for the school to reopen, my Sanskrit teacher mentioned that it was hard to learn a language in a month, but she said, "Let's see if this child can learn this language in a month." I heard this statement from my teacher and considered it an opportunity to prove myself.

When my teacher introduced this beautiful language, I was surprised by Sanskrit's simplicity and the ease with which I read and wrote sentences. I began loving Sanskrit more than my mother tongue. Later, I was admitted into the school and began scoring highest in Sanskrit in my class most of the time. However, I did not know that Sanskrit would change my life over the years to come.

Years went by, and I carried the baggage of self-doubt wherever I went and in whatever I did. I managed to complete my master's, got a job in a reputed multinational institution, and also, got married. Twelve years ago, on a Wednesday afternoon, on my way to my cubicle in my office, I felt my whole body collapse. I had no control of myself, and I held on to a chair so I wouldn't fall.

Something was not right with my body, and with the help of some of my colleagues, I managed to reach home. I used to work for 12 hours a day even after the birth of my first child. I had to return to work 2 months after my delivery. As it was the time of a global recession, I did not want to quit my job and agreed to work on a project that required me to be in the office for longer hours. Leaving my two-month-old baby with my mother, I suffered severe emotional stress. I completely denied my body and mind until my body put a hard break on me.

Sharp shooting pain radiated all over my body from my head to my toes. The pain was so intense that I felt like I was lying on a bed of thorns. My whole body was dysfunctional with acute giddiness, numbness in my fingers and toes, and stomach issues. I was unable to carry out the simplest chore of brushing my teeth or combing my hair. I was unable to travel to work without a cervical collar around my neck as the slightest jerk from applying the brake would hurt me badly. Day by day the pain was aggravated, making it intolerable for me to go to work.

I reached out for support by consulting various physicians and was diagnosed with acute cervical spondylosis. Five out of seven vertebrae in my neck were degenerated. The physicians laid down their hands and said that even a spine surgery would not be able to bring me back to normal health.

I was completely shattered when I heard the news. I came back home disappointed, helpless, and shameful. Quietly, I went to my bed and lay down due to the severe pain of not knowing what to do. It was then my mother came near me and asked me a very profound question: "Do you want to lie down in this pathetic condition as a sympathetic figure forever, or do you want to get back to life?"

This question hit me hard. I did not say anything out loud, but inside me, a loud voice screamed, "No, I don't want to give up now."

I began deeply reflecting on my life experiences and the emotional suffering that I was going through. After many days of deep reflection, I realized that the physical pain that I was going through was a manifestation of the accumulation of the emotions that I had suppressed from my past. This realization made me understand that I was responsible for my own pain and suffering. However, that did not solve my physical pain.

As my family and I were not mentally prepared to go through a spine surgery, we began exploring alternate therapies available around us.

When each door before me closed and all my attempts failed, my heart began to slowly surrender. Deep within me the urge to recover became stronger.

A few days later, I received a phone call from my mother's friend. During the conversation, he asked, as a last resort, if I would like to consult Swami Nirmalananda Giri who was a very well-known spiritual master, naturopathy expert, and expert in treating chronic ailments. With a little bit of hope left in my mind, I went to meet Swamiji. Swamiji looked at me empathetically and said, "Will you be able to follow the procedure, medication, and diet that I prescribe every day and share your weekly progress with me?" Without a second thought, I nodded and agreed to follow. Swamiji's considerate nature, unconditional love, encouragement, support, and medication began working on my weak nerves, slowly making them stronger and stronger every day. In 10 months, I recovered completely and came back to my normal health condition. However, my emotional pain remained as a deep scar on my heart.

I wanted to find an answer to overcome my emotional pain. So I set out on a new journey to discover the answer without any clue where I would end up. Like a hungry man who will eat whatever he finds around, I began searching for the answers in books, spiritual lectures, videos, and mentors.

My quest to know the answer to the question "Where is peace?" grew stronger in me.

Many months later, my mother expressed an interest in meeting an enlightened spiritual master, "Sri M," at his abode in India. We booked a one-on-one meeting with the great Yogi and set out for the trip in the morning. We arrived in a few hours and waited in the garden to be called in. I was excited and, at the same time, nervous inside. After a few minutes, the Yogi's personal assistant called us inside his room. We went into the quiet and calm room where the Yogi was seated. As a way of showing my respect, I bowed before him and sat on the floor. As soon as he saw me sitting on the floor he said, "Please sit in the chair." This small gesture of treating everyone equally changed my perspective about spirituality. Sir's kind gesture, simplicity, and sharp eyes filled with love and understanding made me feel like I was at home. With a wide smile he greeted us and spoke softly as he inquired more about us. I sat like a child with my mouth wide open with curiosity and burning questions in my mind. Before I uttered my questions, he answered them one by one. Time flew in his presence, and I experienced an unexplainable awe, joy, and content within. I am not able to reveal the special advice he offered me. However, I will share one piece of his advice that had a profound impact on me: implement what the teacher has taught rather than worshiping the image of the teacher.

Later, as I was about to leave, he asked me if there was anything else that I would like to ask him. I told him, "I am not happy with the job that I do now, and it does not bring meaning to my life. I feel stuck and want to do something that fulfills my heart." He listened with understanding and asked, "What would that be?" The quick response jumped from my mouth: teaching. He smiled and said, "Everything will be taken care of. God bless." I bowed down before him with deep contentment. Our allocated time for the meeting was over, and the personal assistant came inside to remind us. So we got up from our seats and bowed again with folded hands to bid him goodbye. Meeting Sri M was a transformational experience for my whole family. The seed of inner peace and change was sown into my heart through Sir's powerful presence and words. Little did I know then the beautiful journey of life that was awaiting me.

After we left, the mesmerizing bliss and joy remained in me for many days. Nothing was visible from outside, but internally, I felt blessed and grateful. I began integrating the advice and practices offered to me with great attention.

A few months later, I quit my job. My husband got a job opportunity overseas that required us to travel to Canada. When the travel plan was finalized, I requested to have a phone conversation with my Guru and shared the delightful news with him. In a composed voice he spoke to me briefly for one minute and said, "God bless."

After moving to Canada, I began volunteering for a kid's program in the public library to get local experience before applying for jobs. It was during the visits to the library that rare gems of great masters like the Dalai Lama, Thich Nhat Hanh, Swami Vivekananda, and Mahatma Gandhi inspired me. Eventually, I realized that merely by reading and accumulating information, nothing much was changing inside me. I was continuing the same old patterns of thinking, action, and behavior. I was not sure where the journey would lead me, but I believed in the words of the masters and I was tired of fighting with my mind, which was filled with negative thoughts, emotions, and memories. I was determined not to give up until I found the answer to peace.

In 2015, after my dear grandfather passed away, I started looking for a job in Canada. I did not want to return to a multinational company; instead, I wanted to explore my passions in music. I applied for a job in a private school in Canada and inquired about the music teacher position. The school's president mentioned that there were no vacancies for music teachers. However, he had a vacancy open for a language teacher. He showed me a flier and asked, "Which language do you know among these?" The language that stood out to me was Sanskrit. He was delighted to hear that as he had been looking for a Sanskrit teacher and had not found one yet. He did a quick interview and took me in for the position of Sanskrit teacher. I was over the moon, and it felt like I was connecting back to an old and dear friend I had lost over the years.

I took the opportunity and began to educate students of all age groups. As I taught the meaning behind the Vedic mantras and slokas from the Holy Bhagavad Gita, a huge shift began happening in my mind. The wisdom conveyed helped me understand that all these scriptures offered simple and powerful techniques to train the mind that would help humankind to overcome suffering. I began to have deeper clarity about my own mind in connection to my life. I began watching my mind closely and started seeing disturbing patterns that made me suffer. I noticed that when my mind was happy, I was happy. When my mind was sad, I was sad. As an exploration, I started applying the techniques mentioned in the Holy Bhagavad Gita to my daily life. This included integrating Reiki, music, Sanskrit mantra chanting, Yoga, meditation, and mindfulness into my daily routine.

Slowly, I noticed my mind was developing a resilient mindset through the mental discipline of consistent practice and commitment to these daily techniques. I then began using some of these skills in my daily interactions at work, with family, and in various situations. I noticed my mind was expanding with love, empathy, and compassion and eventually navigating to peace, guiding me towards the next phase of sharing ancient wisdom. Meanwhile, I also got into an IT job in a start-up where there was a lot of flexibility, support, and freedom to express my potential to the fullest.

In 2020, when COVID-19 hit, the school closed for in-person classes. This was when I had the idea to start online classes in Sanskrit. Although many people in my circle knew about Sanskrit, few knew how to read and understand the meaning conveyed through the mantras and slokas in various ancient scriptures. To help my students understand the logical reason behind chanting mantras and the grammatical constructs of the language, I began teaching the Holy Bhagavad Gita in connection to life.

Eight students signed up to learn from me. It was when I was teaching the second chapter of the Holy Bhagavad Gita that one student asked me a challenging question on gaining self-control over temptation. I gave him an answer, mentioning that the desire in us is what triggers temptation when we encounter objects or people.

After responding, I noticed that my students needed help implementing self-control into their daily lives, although they understood it theoretically. I began reflecting deeply on how to bring internal transformation into others' lives.

Three months passed and I was not able to crack the code of how I could bring inner change to others' lives. So I decided to reach out to my coaches and mentors , Roger Burnley and Dr Vincenzo Aliberti to guide me. Through their amazing guidance Vince began coaching sessions with me, and after 3 months, the answer to the question of my life's purpose dawned on me: coaching. As this answer seemed very close to my heart, without doubt I enrolled into the Jay Shetty Certification School. This paved my way to becoming a Jay Shetty Certified Life and Success Coach to help other people dealing with emotional pain to develop a stable mindset and discover peace by integrating ancient wisdom–based tools into my coaching sessions. I also decided to share the knowledge I acquired from ancient wisdom worldwide, which led me to launch Sanskrit courses on the Udemy platform that has benefited nearly 10,000 students across 139 countries.

Today, I feel deeply grateful to be able to help women discover their authentic selves and establish a peaceful family. The many hands of my family, mentors, teachers, and coaches molded me into who I am today. I bow down before all these amazing influencers and situations that have worked in my favor to create this beautiful transformation in my life. This transformation has led me to establish an online school for emotional wellness called Samsarga and to host *The Peace Bridge Podcast* on VoiceAmerica. The most important moral of my story is that we can rise from our pain to discover our peace and purpose in life if we build a resilient mindset and are ready to change and transform our lives.

The ancient wisdom–based tools laid the foundation to enable me to develop self-management skills and emotional resilience, establish healthy work and family relationships, build focus, overcome trauma and limited beliefs, improve my productivity, and remain centered in peace.

Through my life's journey as an IT professional, a Jay Shetty Certified Life and Success Coach, a Sanskrit instructor on Udemy, a Reiki Master, a music teacher, a speaker, a blogger on Core Spirit and Medium, and a podcaster, I believe that if our minds are on our side, centered in peace, then anything in this world is possible.

We don't have to run around in search of peace in the outside world. Instead, we have to turn within and discover more about ourselves, including our own limitations, weaknesses, and strengths. By doing that, we will be able to understand more about our minds, gaining control over and using them properly to live as a warrior in this world.

No pain, no gain.

"Peace comes from within. Do not seek it without." - Gautama Buddha

Through this book, I look forward to sharing the lessons learned in my life from my personal experiences, mentors, coaches, scriptures, and coaching clients to enable one to rise from one's emotional pain and discover peace in life.

CHAPTER 1

PAIN AND SUFFERING

"Our pain can be our greatest teacher. It leads us to places we'd never go on our own."

- Debbie Ford

THE ORIGIN OF PAIN

SINCE THE BEGINNING OF HUMANKIND, pain and suffering have been an integral part of the world. We suffer from pain of different kinds, including mental and physical pain emerging from our physical environment, relationships, trauma, abuse, and much more. Although physical pain heals over time, emotional and mental pain take longer to heal. We usually tend immediately to our physical pain as we consider it more important to treat than emotional pain. So we typically don't run to a doctor to treat our emotional pain seriously unless it has turned into a severe mental health disorder that is beginning to impact our lives.

I did the same with my emotional pain, too. I believed that over time people and situations around me would fix themselves. It was a habit for me to think that if something went wrong at home or in my workplace, it was my fault. I always blamed myself for situations or people not working in my favor. This feeling of not being enough gave rise to the pain of emotional stress and anxiety, causing me to believe that doing something or being like someone else would solve my problems. I did not like myself because I saw myself through the eyes of the people who rejected or disapproved of me. This bag of pain grew much more extensive with time and was triggered when I met similar people in my workplace or family. My sensitivity to people and situations grew to the point where I thought avoidance would be a quick way to solve it. So I began avoiding it by changing jobs or moving to a different city. However, to my wonder, I noticed the same type of people and situations that hurt me emotionally would appear in another form, and I was back to my emotional suffering again.

This never-ending emotional breakdown cycle was tiring and painful.

I would sit and cry for hours, not knowing how to fix it, or distract myself by listening to music, watching a movie, or going shopping. However, when the distraction ended, and the same situation returned, I would return to square one again and suffer. This continued and I began to try a different approach by sharing my pain with my family and friends. They would listen and then tell me, "You know that you should have done this. It is because you did this that this happened . . ." and so on. The more I shared, the more my pain further increased. All the little tricks that I knew did not work to rescue me from my emotional pain.

The word *pain* usually brings us a feeling of discomfort that moves us away from a place of happiness. It often comes uninvited during the most unexpected times.

According to medical professionals, pain is often considered a symptom of an underlying problem.

Pain can show up as physical or mental, arising from 7 dimensions that include spiritual, cognitive, affective, behavioral, physical, sensory, and sociocultural.

Most often, we take proactive actions to deal with physical pain. When we have unbearable physical pain like a headache or stomach ache, we may reach for an over-the-counter drug to relieve our pain. However, with emotional pain, the quick fixes will only suppress the pain and not resolve the underlying issue. So we usually pay less attention to our mental and emotional pain and live with it for years unless it bothers us deeply.

TYPES OF PAIN

Pain can be classified into avoidable and unavoidable pain.

Unavoidable pain refers to the pain we experience due to natural disasters, death, or illness. This category of pain does not happen every day of our lives but is occasional.

Avoidable pain refers to pain that is caused by our own mind and its interactions with the world around us through our relationships. It is avoidable because it is based on our perceptions of the situations and people around us. When our avoidable pain moves to a dimension where our happiness, freedom, and peace are affected, we suffer due to the pain.

Avoiding, ignoring, or suppressing emotional pain is not a permanent solution to pain management.

As our brain stores memories from past events, it also retains memories of the pain we have endured. This pain, stored in each cell within our body, can be triggered when similar events occur in our lives, leaving us in a place of self-doubt, shame, anger, guilt, regret, and resentment and causing us more pain.

When we do not manage our emotional pain properly, it leads to chronic mental and physical health issues over time. It also impacts our identity, self-esteem, relationships, and performance, preventing us from being able to lead an authentic life with freedom and self-expression.

According to ancient wisdom, there are 3 different kinds of pain that human beings go through in life, which include:

1. Adhyatmika—pain that causes fear, anxiety, worry, and self-doubt due to physical, emotional, or mental pain
2. Adhibhautika—pain arising from relationships
3. Adhidaivika—pain due to natural calamities

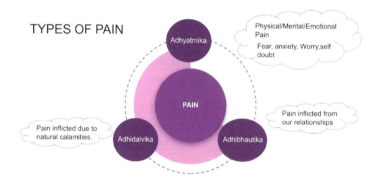

Adhyatmika (emotional pain):
1. Worry
2. Self-doubt
3. Fear
4. Anxiety
5. Insecurity
6. Sorrow
7. Anger
8. Shame
9. Guilt

We usually don't call them pain until we experience these emotions and the emotional distress takes away peace and happiness from our lives.

We may get stuck in the emotions and suffer repeatedly, not knowing a way out. In this helpless state, the emotional pain is so hard to bear and causes further harm to ourselves. It is like getting trapped in a self-inflicted cage.

For example, stress-induced emotions can lead to anxiety, overthinking, or rumination whenever we cannot cope with challenging people or situations.

This pain neither benefits us nor others around us.

According to Patanjali's *Yoga Sutras*,[2] the main causes of this type of pain and suffering that we go through in our life are classified into the categories of ignorance, ego, attachment, desire, and aversion.

CHANGING YOUR PERSPECTIVE

We experience pain because we are consumed by our emotions, which constantly change as we create these emotions. We are the creators of our emotional suffering, too.

As we have been taught to avoid our pain, we consider it wrong to go through it. So we try our best not to get into a place of despair as much as possible. Happiness is the ideal state we all love to be in. When anything disturbs our happiness, we get into states of agitation projected by our mind through various emotions. Our reactions to our pain are based on our previous experiences and beliefs or perspectives towards it.

Your emotional pain is a symptom of an underlying problem that needs immediate attention, requiring you to take action.

---

2   Patanjali, "Samadhi Pada."

Approach pain not as a problem but instead as a good friend who has come to offer you a lesson so that you can work on the area and move forward in your life.

Changing our perspective towards pain determines our suffering. When we look at pain rationally and utilize the lesson, we can use it for personal growth and well-being. It can also help us develop emotional strength and tap into our inner wisdom, which is essential in leading a peaceful life.

When we change our perspective of our pain, we can channel our energy positively and overcome our suffering. The way to do that lies in accepting it, taking steps towards healing it, and learning from it.

Humans are gifted with infinite potential and can rise above our pain and suffering anytime. The power and choice are in us.

My emotional pain propelled me to discover inner peace and well-being. It directed me towards learning more about rising from pain through connecting with spiritual mentors, coaches, and books. It made me learn and integrate various spiritual tools into my daily routine to develop mental discipline. It made me understand that my ego is powerless and deepened my faith to surrender to God. It made me empathize with the sufferings of others and led me to carry out my life's purpose through coaching with compassion towards other beings in the world. Ultimately, it is the secret sauce that built resilience in me.

If I had not experienced emotional pain, I would not have made efforts to navigate out of it.

The deeper the pain, the deeper our urge to rise above it.

As no change is permanent, no pain is endless. So please don't run away from it or ignore it with temporary fixes. Instead, take action to transform your pain into resilience, compassion, empathy, and love that can empower you to lead a peaceful life.

Turn your pain into your true power.

Pain brings suffering, but accepting it becomes the fuel to discover your purpose and peace in life.

Find some time to sit with your pain to determine the source. Sometimes, it could be hard to find it by yourself, and that is why it might require consulting with a therapist or a coach to help you sort it out so that it is easier for you to take necessary steps to move forward in life.

REFLECTIONS

1. What type of pain do you have the most in your life? (Pain from relationships, emotional pain, etc.)
2. When do you experience the most emotional pain?
3. What have you tried to relieve your emotional pain?

CHAPTER 2
VEHICLE

"You either control the mind, or the mind controls you."
- Napoleon Hill

From our childhood days, we have been taught to take care of our bodies and physical health, follow social etiquette and behave well before others, learn, and excel to find good jobs to earn a living. However, why are we still unable to find peace in our lives despite having a good family, house, food, employment, and more? We tend to neglect the health of our minds and look at fixing people and situations outside us. The more we look at blaming the external world, the more we become unconscious about our minds that are left unaltered for years.

Based on Maslow's hierarchy of needs,[3] there are 5 different needs that humans look for. The first is physiological needs, which refer to food, water, sleep, clothing, reproduction, and air. Next comes safety needs, including employment, personal security, property, and physical health. After this comes love and belonging, which refers to friendship, family, and connections. The 4th need is esteem, which relates to respect, recognition, freedom, and status. Only when we have all 4 needs can we progress towards the

---

3   Mcleod, "Maslow's Hierarchy of Needs."

5th need, self-actualization, which means the desire to realize one's true potential.

Let's take a moment now to assess where you are in the hierarchy of physiological needs, safety, love and belonging, esteem, and self-actualization.

Most of us do not reach self-actualization because we are stuck between the 1st and 4th levels.

INTELLECTUAL QUOTIENT VS. EMOTIONAL QUOTIENT

We are all born unique with infinite potential. However, various factors can influence our personalities as we grow up, including our environment, other people, and situations. Our characters are derived from our level of intelligence, which includes IQ and EQ (Emotional Quotient).

IQ refers to that part of the brain that helps us to learn, accumulate, and reproduce information. In contrast, EQ refers to the part of the brain that allows us to handle challenges, adapt to changes, manage stress and emotions, communicate effectively, and more. We focus only on developing IQ in our life and then end up unable to address real-life problems as we have never been taught to develop EQ. So we enter real life unprepared to face challenges that require us to manage ourselves and the world around us. This leads us to a helpless state where we are left with options to ignore, give up, or deal with them effectively. Some of us rely on people to escape from reality, fall into addictions, change our environment, consume drugs, immerse ourselves in social media, and much more. Although they all provide temporary relief, none of these have the ability or power to give the peace of mind that our minds are seeking for.

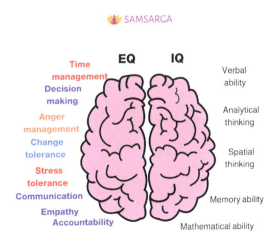

The peace we seek can only be obtained when our minds are quiet and free from chattering. The noises in our mind are created from our thoughts that emerge from our external environment through our 5 sense organs and the accumulation of memories and tendencies from our past. These noises strongly influence our emotions, actions, and behavior. So when we allow different kinds of noises into our minds and let them all play inside us, we experience various feelings and act based on them. This disturbs not only our minds but also our bodies.

For example, let's take the case of the negative emotion of anger. When we are angry, certain parts of our brain activate, including the amygdala, which activates the hypothalamus that sends signals to the corresponding pituitary. The adrenal gland secretes hormones as chemicals into the bloodstream, which eventually impacts various organs in our body and causes chronic diseases that affect the cardiovascular, respiratory, neurological, and endocrine systems. This can take the form of heart attacks, diabetes, compromised immunity, anxiety, depression, mental and behavioral disorders, and more.

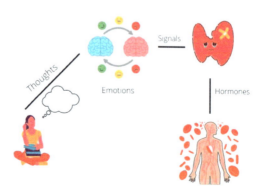

We then rely on drugs to help our bodies recover, but the root cause remains unattended. Not everything our minds think is true. We often allow our mind to create its drama with the help of our imaginations, beliefs, and memories, which we most often don't realize. This eventually leads to a place of mental suffering designed by ourselves.

Let me share a famous Zen story[4] with you. Long ago, 2 monks were traveling together. At one point, they came to a river, which was flowing very strongly. As they prepared to cross the river, they saw a very young and pretty woman trying to cross the river. The young woman sought their help to cross to the other side of the river.

The 2 monks were confused and looked at one another. They had taken vows that they would never touch a woman.

All of a sudden, the older monk picked up the pretty woman and carried her on his shoulders across the river. After crossing the river, he placed her gently on the shore and carried on with his journey.

The younger monk was speechless as he could not believe what had just happened. He rejoined his companion, and there were no words exchanged for an hour.

After a few hours and unable to contain his urge, the younger monk asked the older monk, "We being monks, we were prohibited from touching women. How could you then carry that woman on your shoulders and help her cross the river?"

The older monk smiled and replied, "My dear brother, I set her down after crossing the river; why are you still carrying her?"

We all also load many webs of memories, ego, and negative emotions like hatred, jealousy, comparison, and sorrow into our minds for many years. This only leads to hurting ourselves and

---

4   KindSpring, "Two Monks and a Woman – A Zen Lesson."

sinking into deep mental pits that prevent us from being authentic and discovering peace in our lives. Unless we unload them from our minds, peace is unachievable.

Our **mind** is a potent weapon that has been gifted to us. It is like a knife that can be used for different purposes. A knife can cut vegetables or kill a person. In the same way, positive emotions of love energize us. In contrast, negative feelings of fear, hatred, and sorrow drain our energy, make us tired, and cause us to develop mental health issues. We often pollute our minds with negative emotions and never realize their impact on us until they manifest as anxiety, depression, and other mental health issues.

The power lies in us to keep the treasure house called the mind clean and healthy.

EMOTIONAL WELLNESS

"Positive and negative emotions cannot occupy our minds at the same time." - Napoleon Hill

We often reach for food or water when we are hungry and thirsty. Hunger and thirst are signals from our body, prompting us to take care of the body's needs. In the same way, our minds also communicate to us through our thoughts and emotions. The mind receives its input provided by our 5 sense organs through our sight, smell, touch, taste, and sound.

Later, the mind processes based on our beliefs and memories. After this process, it generates thoughts. The thoughts we carry have energy based on the intention offered by us. The mind can cause positive or negative thoughts based on the beliefs we entertain.

For example, seeing a bee triggers a thought of fear based on memories of bees recorded in your brain that inform you that bees can hurt and cause pain. So as soon as we see a bee near us, thoughts of fear flood us followed by feelings of anxiety. Our body and mind then take action based on our thoughts, beliefs, and feelings. Naturally driven by that thought, we take corresponding steps like moving away from the place or trying to kill the bee. This way, our entire behavior is formed.

Most often, we unconsciously perform actions based on the communications from our minds. However, emotions and thoughts are our mind's mechanism to communicate with us.

Our responsibility is to regulate our minds in the right path through the power of discrimination. If we closely observe our minds, we will notice that no emotion or thoughts stay forever. They keep changing every minute. Like in a movie, different scenes come and go within our minds. When we are controlled by our overpowered desires and emotions, we act based on them without reflection and discrimination, leading to chaos. Our mind is the vehicle that can take us to the destination of peace. However, it requires us to be a driver to steer it in the right direction.

Regulating our thoughts and emotions is the key to emotional wellness.

Our well-being consists of 8 dimensions. This includes physical, occupational, social, spiritual, intellectual, environmental, financial, and emotional.

Among these, emotional well-being plays a significant role in our mental health.

An article published in the National Institute of Health defines emotional wellness as coping with life stressors and adapting to change, even in difficult times.[5]

---

5   National Institutes of Health, "Emotional Wellness Toolkit."

Some signs of poor emotional health include:

- Feeling exhausted or burned out most of the time
- Sleeplessness or sleeping too much
- Poor performance at work
- Feeling anxious or irritated with loved ones
- No time for self-care
- Physical symptoms of stress, like high blood pressure or heart palpitations
- Low confidence or low self-esteem

Developing good emotional health helps us to manage our thinking, emotions, and actions, as well as increases our emotional intelligence, leading us to a place of self-resilience and peace.

It is possible to develop emotional wellness in our lives because our brains have been gifted with the power of neuroplasticity, which means we can create new neural pathways within our brains by reprogramming our thinking and behavior.

Developing our emotional intelligence is one of the ways to achieve this emotional wellness that leads to resilience and peace.

According to Daniel Goleman, the 4 essential areas within emotional intelligence are self-awareness, self-management, relationship management, and social awareness.

Among these, if we can manage ourselves, we can solve 90% of the problems in our life.

This means that if we gain self-mastery by regulating our minds, we can lead a peaceful life regardless of our circumstances.

The path to this self-mastery is prescribed by Great Rishis in ancient wisdom that consists of the Vedas, Upanishads, The Holy Bhagavad Gita, and more.

REFLECTION

1. Which level of Maslow's hierarchy are you currently in?
2. What are some of the signs of emotional health issues that you have noticed so far?
3. What EQ skills would help you improve your emotional health?
4. What are some of the positive and negative emotions that you experience the most in your day-to-day life?

CHAPTER 3

PERSPECTIVE FROM ANCIENT WISDOM

"Spirituality is the science of the soul."
- Swami Vivekananda

SPIRITUALITY

CAN SPIRITUALITY HELP SOLVE MODERN life problems?

Every day in our life, we come across various life challenges at home, work, and many other places. However, we are not taught skills at school or at home that can help us face life's challenges; instead, we are taught to develop skills that will help us earn a living. Although we need to earn to live, that alone cannot help sustain our life.

Most of us enter real life without knowing how to deal with tough situations and people in our life. Over the years, some of us learn from people, books or podcasts, and life experiences and gain skills that make us better prepared, whereas some others struggle to achieve the necessary resilience.

Resilience is a state of mind where we are able to face life situations, good or bad, by managing our emotions and thoughts effectively.

The word *spiritual* does not mean being religious. Religion is a set of beliefs and customs, whereas spirituality is beyond religion and refers to an elevated way of living.

Mere reading of scriptures and acquiring knowledge does not make one spiritual and bring internal transformation. This is one of the reasons that we see a lot of people who have read various scriptures and listened to different spiritual talks remain the same person because the accumulated knowledge from the scriptures has not been applied to their life, bringing into alignment the way they speak, think, and act. When you lack this harmony, it creates internal conflict and makes you live a pretentious life on the outside, while you suffer inside.

Our minds continue fluctuating back and forth until we are tired and deeply desire to find the way to get out of this drama. True spirituality gives us the mental and emotional strength to withstand the problems and challenges that we face in our lives. We can become spiritual only when we are able to elevate ourselves from the place of ego and internal struggles with our thoughts and emotions that prevent us from being our true self with infinite potential.

All the knowledge in the world and all the teachings from the great spiritual masters can give us direction in our life's journey. However, to awaken ourselves to a place where we can love and serve others as we serve ourselves, we need to take charge of our minds and do the internal work.

Each one of us is unique and has immense potential within us. We all have a spark of divinity that is the higher self or higher intelligence. However, this is clouded by our upbringing and various interactions with the world. We have forgotten who we truly are and lead a life under the mercy of our situations and people around us. Sometimes we are sad. Sometimes we are happy. Sometimes we are excited. Sometimes we are angry.

When our mind controls us through our negative thoughts and emotions, it becomes very hard for us to tap into our true self and act from our true inner core or center.

The centered state is a state where you have self-control, or control over your own mind, wherein we are able to use it effectively rather than allowing the mind to use us. Through this process, you will be able to channel your energies in the right direction to help you achieve your goals, improve your focus and productivity, as well as live a peaceful and happy life.

In order to achieve this elevated state, it is necessary to train and channel your mind so that it can perform at its maximum capacity.

Ancient Rishis knew that no material knowledge has the power to train our minds to tap into the higher intelligence in us. So they discovered and shared various powerful tools to train our minds that we can use in the form of meditations, mantras, Yoga, breathing techniques, and more. We will be looking into some of these powerful tools.

Although these powerful tools have the capability to transform our lives holistically, they do not make a huge impact in our lives unless we have the right internal mental setup.

The internal setup is an essential qualification for a spiritual seeker in the ancient text *Atma Bodha*[6] by Shankaracharya described below.

FOUR D's OF SPIRITUAL QUALIFICATIONS

1. Viveka—discrimination
2. Vairagya—detachment

6   Vedanta Students, https://vedantastudents.com.

3. Shad Sampath—discipline -6 virtues of inner wealth
4. Mumukshutva—desire or yearning for freedom from clutches of the mind (liberation from emotional and mental bondages)

4 QUALIFICATIONS
OF A SPIRITUAL SEEKER

DESIRE	DISCIPLINE	DISCRIMINATION	DETACHMENT
Desire to Change	Mental discipline	Discriminate right and wrong	Detach mentally from actions, people and events

Tatva Bodha - Sri Adi Shankaracharya

The Shad Sampath, or 6 virtues, prescribed in chapter 6 of the book *Spiritual Aspiration and Practice*[7] are:

1. **Sama**—control of the mind
2. **Dama**—control of the senses
3. **Uparati**—withdrawal from sense organs
4. **Titiksha**—accepting situations without negative reactions
5. **Sraddha**—faith in scriptures and the Guru's words
6. **Samadhana**—contentment through equanimity of mind

---

7   Krishnananda, "Sadhana Chatushtaya."

6 VIRTUES OF INNER WEALTH

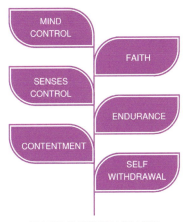

MIND CONTROL

FAITH

SENSES CONTROL

ENDURANCE

CONTENTMENT

SELF WITHDRAWAL

SRI ADI SHANKARACHARYA

Except the desire to change and faith, all the other qualifications mentioned above represent self-management skills that can be learned, cultivated, and enhanced with proper guidance, willpower, consistency, and practice. The reason I say this with confidence is because these 4 D's have been the core pillars that have enabled me to strengthen my mindset to develop peace, stability, and resilience in my life.

A peaceful mind is the path to excellence.

Only when the veil of mental agitation is lifted will we be able to think clearly and live as the glorious higher intelligence shining and radiating its true divinity around.

The ultimate aim of spirituality is to help us:

• Attain internal freedom and peace
• Stabilize mental health
• Rise above our lower tendencies, negative thinking and emotions, ego, and selfish desires

- Discover our true higher self
- Lead a conscious, authentic, and balanced life with an aligned body and mind
- Tap into the higher intelligence and wisdom within us
- Channel our energies in the right direction to live a purposeful life

Elevating your mind is the first step towards peace. In order to elevate your mind, it is important to understand the constitution of your mind, its qualities and states that influence your behavior so that you can recognize and train it effectively during your day.

FOUR DIVISIONS OF THE MIND

Based on the ancient scripture Patanjali's *Yoga Sutras*, our minds are divided into 4 parts and referred to as the Antahkarana, meaning "the instrument."[8]

MANAS—represents a bundle of thoughts. It can be imagined as a river which keeps flowing with good and bad objects thrown into it. The good and bad things thrown in are the thoughts and emotions that never stay the same and come and go every moment.

BUDDHI—represents intelligence that is based on logic, reasoning, and decision-making.

CHITTA—represents the memories of our past experiences that we have recorded and used as references whenever we encounter new situations.

AHAMKARA—refers to ego, which brings the connection to "I" into every action, relationship, and interaction we have. For example, everything that you say using *me* and *mine* is from ego.

---

8   Patanjali, "Samadhi Pada."

All these parts cannot work without the power supply that comes from the **Atman**, called in different names as the awareness or consciousness or higher intelligence. This consciousness is the watcher who is awake while you are in sleep or in a dream state.

Most of us, when we are unconscious during our day, identify ourselves based on our thoughts, intelligence, memory, or ego. However, our true personality is that of the higher self that operates all 4 parts of our body every day even when we are unaware.

The higher self in all of us is the spirit of higher intelligence that has infinite potential, has the power to answer all our questions, is a source of wisdom, and can guide us in the right path if we follow it.

Connecting to the higher self gives us the strength to believe in ourselves, trust the inner voice, and lead a happy and peaceful life.

The higher self has no religion and is all knowing, not bound by space or time.

When we live our life aligned to the inner wisdom, we bring out the best potential in us.

A famous analogy of 2 birds sitting in a tree is shared in the *Mundaka Upanishad* to help us understand this concept. According to the analogy, the 2 birds live on the same tree. One bird sits on the lower branch and the other on a higher branch. The bird on the lower branch hops to different branches on the tree, tasting the fruits to find the sweeter ones, whereas the bird on the higher branch silently watches the bird on the lower branch without hopping around for the fruits. The bird on the lower branch is the lower self that wanders around the world for pleasures to satisfy its own desires, whereas the bird on the higher branch represents the Atman, or true higher self, as the aware conscience. The tree represents our body that has the lower and higher self regardless of whether we are a man or woman.

In our life, like the bird on the lower branch, we are attracted to various things in the world in our search for happiness and to satisfy our desires, and we do not realize that what we are searching for is not something to be found outside but within.

There is a famous text written by the great sage Shankaracharya called "Nirvana Shatakam," which describes the pure self that is neither the body, the mind, or the intellect nor is it the actions performed by us. True self is the pure consciousness that is free from likes and dislikes, pleasure and pain, praise and criticism that remains the same at all times.

To lead a life where you are acting from the identity of the Atman, or self, requires you to be able to purify the different layers of the mind.

When the river keeps flowing with a lot of dirt, it is impossible to see the pebbles and beautiful rocks under it. However, on a calm and serene lake, we can easily see through the stones, sand, and gravel.

Similarly, it is only when our minds become calm and peaceful that we can let the Atman shine through us. Otherwise, we will be in the control of our thoughts, emotions, and beliefs that will keep us stuck in the Manas layer forever.

A famous story about Buddha describes the nature of a calm mind.[9]

Once, Buddha was traveling the forest with his disciples.

As they were passing a lake, Buddha expressed to one of his disciples his desire to have some water. The disciple went to the lake to fetch some water. At the very same time, a bullock cart crossed through the lake, and the water became dirty.

---

9   Anonymous, "Muddy Water (Wisdom, Buddha)," *Stories From All Around the World*, *WordPress*.

Seeing this the disciple thought, *How can I give this dirty water to my master to drink?*

So he returned to his master and told him, "The water is very dirty and hence is not fit for drinking."

After a few minutes, Buddha asked the same disciple to return to the lake and fetch some water.

The disciple went and found that the water was still dirty. He returned and told his master that it was still muddy and hence not fit to drink. After some time, Buddha asked the same disciple again to go and fetch some water. This time, the disciple found the dirt had settled down, and the water was clean. So he collected some water in a pot and brought it to his master. Buddha looked at the water and said, "See what you did to clean the water. When you let the dirt settle down on its own you got clear water."

Your mind is like that, too! When it is disturbed, it is muddy. When it is calm, it is peaceful.

The different divisions of our mind that cause disturbances need to be purified for the higher self to shine through you.

IMPURITIES OF THE MIND

According to Patanjali's *Yoga Sutras*, the 6 most common impurities that cause disturbances in the mind are due to:

6 STEALERS OF PEACE

LUST

PRIDE

ANGER

DELUSION

GREED

JEALOUSY

ANCIENT WISDOM

- **Kama** (Lust)
- **Krodha** (Anger)
- **Lobha** (Greed)

- **Moha** (Delusion)
- **Mada** (Pride)
- **Matsarya** (Envy)

These impurities can emerge from our own beliefs and selfish desires.

BELIEFS

As discussed in the second chapter, "Vehicle," our beliefs are one of the sources of our thoughts, emotions, and behaviors. Beliefs are impressions from our past experiences recorded in our brains that provide an easy mechanism to process information from the world and equip us to take action. These beliefs act as our internal lens through which we make assumptions and judgments. We derive beliefs the moment we are born from our parents, teachers, friends, culture, religion, and more.

Not all beliefs are bad. Beliefs that disturb our inner peace and peace around the world fall under the category of limiting beliefs. The definition of a limiting belief is a thought or state of mind that you think is the absolute truth and that stops you from doing certain things.

We have all been gifted infinite intelligence and limitless minds. However, we see the world through our little magnifying lens made up of our beliefs, biases, prejudices, memories, and conditioning from our past. Over the years, we form a habit of sending misinterpreted data conceived through our perceptions to our brain and mind, which eventually leads us to limited thinking and behavior. Some of us hardly pay attention to this as we have been accustomed to leading an unconscious life as we follow the same habits of thinking from our childhood and remain in our comfort zone where we are not required to make the smallest change in our mindset. We defend our beliefs and justify them. This prevents us from tapping into our infinite potential and realizing our authentic power.

Limiting beliefs are inner barriers that limit us from viewing ourselves and the world around us in a truthful way.

Limiting beliefs can show up in 3 forms:

1. **SELF**—Limiting beliefs in ourselves arise from how we perceive ourselves and the stories we tell ourselves every day. It gives rise to self-sabotage of various kinds that show up in the form of self-doubt, procrastination, perfectionism, impostor syndrome, and eventually, anxiety and depression. They also impact our relationships at work, with our family, children, or parents, and more. A few examples of limited beliefs are statements like: "I am not enough;" "I am a failure;" "I can't do this;" "I am judged;" "I am ridiculed;" and more.

2. **PEOPLE** - Limiting beliefs about people lead us to form judgments, prejudices, and biases, labeling them as good or bad based on religion, race, culture, country, and more. This belief is what leads to acts of bullying, humiliation, hatred, racism, enmity, and wars.

3. **LIFE**—Limiting beliefs about life lead us to make generalizations about life. For example, we make generalizations about happiness, success, time, and more. A few statements that arise would be: "I don't have time;" "Life is unfair;" and "Success is not for everyone."

It is unfortunate that education has not helped us to re-educate our hearts to break free from the barriers of limited beliefs. Unless we break free from this pattern, peace is unachievable.

A coach or mentor plays a key role in helping us overcome our limited beliefs that are present in our subconscious mind.

A long time ago, a pregnant lion gave birth to a cub and passed away. The newborn cub walked around and found a herd of sheep. It began mingling with them, and the mother sheep decided to raise it as her own.

The lion grew up with other sheep and started thinking and acting just like them. It would eat grass and bleat like them.

However, it sometimes felt left out.

The sheep would say, "You look different from us and have a strange voice. Why can't you become like us? You don't belong to our community!"

The lion would listen to these remarks and feel sad. It felt that by being different it was bringing disgrace to the sheep community.

Many days went by, and an old lion in the forest noticed these sheep and decided to attack them. As it chased the sheep, the old lion's attention fell on the little lion.

The older lion stopped chasing and wondered why the younger lion was among the sheep. In surprise, it growled at the little lion and asked why it was with the sheep.

The younger lion responded in fear, "Please leave me. I am a young sheep."

The older lion growled loudly and said, "Are you crazy? You are a lion just like me!"

The younger lion again said, "I am a sheep. Leave me alone."

The old lion dragged the little lion to a river nearby and told it to look at its reflection.

When the young lion looked at its reflection, it was astonished and saw that it was not a sheep but a mighty lion!

After realizing the truth, the young lion growled courageously. The powerful growling reached all parts of the forest, and all the sheep began to hide behind the bushes and run away from the young lion.

The sheep that made fun of the lion became too scared to come close to the lion that had realized its true nature.

MORAL OF THE STORY

In our lives, the older lion could be a coach, mentor, or teacher who enables us to see our true reflection of the higher self by offering us guidance, tools, and support to overcome the limiting beliefs that are holding us back, preventing us from living a life of freedom and choice.

When the younger lion becomes aware of its limiting beliefs through self-reflection it realizes its true nature. It is no longer influenced by its surroundings and showcases its authentic self.

Just like the younger lion in this story, you might have been brought up in surroundings that were negative, and hence, you have accumulated many negative beliefs about yourself. Bad parenting, bad teachers, bad peers, media, government, and society can all have these negative influences on us when we are young.

As an adult, it is easy to lose yourself in negative thoughts and to start feeling like a victim by blaming the past. But that will only keep you stuck in the current reality. To change your reality and find your tribe, you need to start working on your inner self and focus all your energy towards becoming self-aware.

The higher self is not an external entity. It is an internal entity. It lives right inside you. Allow your awareness to shine light onto all your limiting beliefs and find who you truly are.

We need to break the walls of limited beliefs and thinking in order to view and perceive the world in its actuality without the colors and shades that we would like to be painted on them. Only then will we be able to expand our thinking and mindset to grow to the best version of ourselves.

Changing ourselves will change the world around us by opening limitless possibilities in and around us.

Next, let's look at the impurity from your own inner tendencies, called vasanas, that give rise to lust, or desires, and prompt you to take respective actions.

VASANAS

All of us are born with good and bad tendencies that are inherited and accumulated from our own past.

These tendencies have the power to impact your behavior through your own thoughts, emotions, and actions. Depending on the tendency, you are attracted to certain kinds of people, objects, and situations in your life. These tendencies exhibit themselves as desires that become thoughts when triggered by our sense organs.

The more we satisfy our vasanas, the more they become robust and more profound.

Vasanas that are driven by our ego are considered impure as they create agitations in our mind, whereas vasanas that leave us energized and peaceful are considered "pure" vasanas.

When we unconsciously behave based on our vasanas, we are driven crazy to do all kinds of things to satisfy them.

Have you ever been to a clothing store and picked up a dress that you saw and felt a strong desire to possess it?

Once you buy the dress, you might feel like the winner of a contest, beating the others in the store who could not purchase it. When you wear it, you might even feel like you are a princess. However, in a few weeks or months, this same dress may lose its charm, and then when you go to the clothing store again, you will find another one that looks more charming. I am not saying that you should not buy clothing and dress up well. What I am trying to convey is, this never-ending, vicious cycle makes you become caught up in believing that material possessions will bring you fulfillment. The dress in itself does not have the power to make you happy forever, and the happiness lasts only till you buy and wear it. Afterward, the happiness fades away. Every time you satisfy the desire, you may notice that the urge does not end and keeps on growing. So this want arises from our vasanas that make you run after things around you. The vasanas cannot be fulfilled by providing it with what it needs because it is like offering a crying kid a toy believing that it will not cry again. Unless the kid is taught to behave properly, it will drain your time and energy to please it. Similarly, only when you train your mind not to run after everything around you will you begin to conserve your focus and energy that can be redirected to utilizing your full potential.

Vasanas are not restricted to objects alone. They can be towards people, animals, plants, and anything that you perceive through your senses—namely sight, sound, smell, taste, and touch—that ignites a desire in you to want and have more.

It is when our desires create strong attachment that we become dependent on them to make us happy all the time. When this goes beyond our control, it turns into addiction.

ध्यायतो विषयान्पुसः सङ्गस्तेषूपजायते ।
सङ्गात्सञ्जायते कामः कामात्क्रोधोऽभिजायते ॥ ६२॥

Dhyayato Vishyan Pumsaha sangasteshu upajayate
Sangath Sanjayate kamaha kamath krodho abhi jayathe[10]

---

10   The Holy Bhagavad Gita 2:62

In the Holy Bhagavad Gita, Lord Krishna tells Arjuna that your contemplation on external objects develops into attachment. This attachment towards it develops anger, eventually leading to misery and destruction.

For example, if you are someone who is undergoing stress and have found temporary relief from drugs, every time you experience stress, you might resort to drugs which will cause you to develop an attachment towards them. When the drug becomes unavailable, it can trigger anger and disappointment.

We all may have different stacks of vasanas, which show up as desire and lead to thought and action.

Three different types of vasanas are usually seen:

1. **Deha vasana**: deepest desire to fulfill your body's needs
2. **Loka vasana**: most profound attachments towards things and people
3. **Shastra vasana**: deepest desire to learn from scriptures and the world around us

As we continue repeating actions based on our inner tendencies, we start developing habits of various kinds that include physical, mental, social, financial, and more.

These habits form neural pathways in the brain that contribute to our behavior. When you are unconscious, your brain relies on these pathways to prompt corresponding actions.

In Charles Duhigg's *The Power of Habit,11* he mentions the pattern of our habits, good or bad, falls into 3 R's that are:

1. **Reminder**—triggers that we receive through our sense organs
2. **Routine**—action that we take based on the triggers

---

11 Duhigg, "The Golden Rule of Habit Change," *The Power of Habit.*

3. **Reward**—result that you get from doing the action

Although some of these vasanas are required for us to survive, it is when impure vasanas grow out of proportion from needs to wants that we lose our balance in life.

We cannot eradicate all our vasanas. The suggested approach in the Holy Bhagavad Gita is to purify the impure vasanas so that they are eventually eliminated.

The process to purify the vasanas includes self-awareness, self-control, detachment, and having an egoless attitude. When you begin establishing these new practices to manage your vasanas, the pathways in your brain are rewired, eventually erasing the old habit patterns.

We will look into these steps in detail in the coming chapters. When the intensity of the pure vasanas supersedes the impure vasanas, our mind begins to slowly settle down to a peaceful state.

Next, let's look at the qualities that we derive based on our vasanas.

THE 3 QUALITIES OF THE MIND

Have you noticed yourself fluctuating between feeling lazy, anxious, and happy during your day?

According to the Holy Bhagavad Gita, we are all born from nature that has 3 qualities or Gunas. We all exhibit the 3 qualities, Satva, Rajas, and Tamas, at different times during our days.

Satva is the state where our minds are harmonious, transparent, peaceful, joyful, and wise.

Rajas is the state of energy, change, action, and movement driven by passion. It is when you carry out your actions from a place of ego with attachment to the results. It leads to restlessness, competition, self-centeredness, anger, anxiety, stress, fear, and worry.

Tamas is the state of inactivity that arises from ignorance. It includes laziness, lethargy, guilt, shame, procrastination, confusion, depression, grief, and lack of self-control.

Each of these qualities, or Gunas, in you carry energy that you express through your thoughts, emotions, and actions, which determine your experience of life.

To raise the mind from the energy of Tamas to Satva, you need to progress through Rajas by performing actions and purifying them. Purifying the actions refers to carrying out positive activities with a selfless attitude.

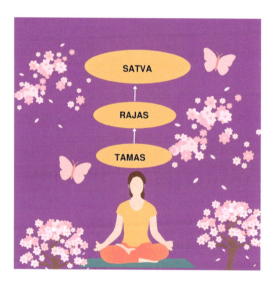

The experience of the world by a person in Tamas is sorrow filled. You can change the experience by altering the qualities of your mind that emerge from your thoughts, incorporating observation and conscious positive action into your life.

The Rajas state is dominated by action and passion that can bring stress and anxiety when done with a selfish motive. This experience can be altered by consciously incorporating detachment (carrying out selfless actions without being attached to the results) and slowing down to reduce the agitation of your mind.

When the energy is elevated from Tamas to Rajas and becomes balanced, Satva arises as calmness, wisdom, and joy.

These Gunas can also be influenced through the food we consume and the people we associate with in our lives.

According to the Holy Bhagavad Gita, sattvic foods are those that bring purity, strength, health, and joy. Rajasic foods are those that are bitter, sour, saline, or excessively hot and can lead to pain, grief, and disease. Tamasic foods are those that are stale, rotten, and tasteless.

You cannot eliminate the Gunas in you nor can you stay in Satva all the time. However, you can develop stability of mind by bringing your attention to the present moment to be conscious of the Guna that you are experiencing and then shift from the existing Guna to your ideal Guna in order to balance these energies.

ACTIVITIES THAT CAN HELP YOU TRANSCEND FROM TAMAS TO RAJAS TO DEVELOP BALANCE

TAMAS	RAJAS
BORED LETHARGIC SAD MOODY LONELY GRIEVING PROCRASTINATING	READ AN INSPIRING BOOK
	LISTEN TO GOOD MUSIC
	CARRY OUT YOUR PASSION
	LISTEN / WATCH MOTIVATIONAL VIDEOS
	WATCH FUNNY SHOWS
	DANCE
	YOGA/WORKOUT
	CONNECT WITH POSITIVE PEOPLE
	HELP SOMEONE

ACTIVITIES THAT CAN HELP YOU TRANSCEND FROM RAJAS TO SATVA TO DEVELOP BALANCE

RAJAS	SATVA
ANGER STRESS ANXIETY WORRY FEAR	BREATHING EXERCISES
	MINDFULNESS EXERCISES
	MEDITATIONS
	YOGA
	GRATITUDE JOURNALING
	SELF-REFLECTION
	LIVING BY VALUES AND PURPOSE
	SELF-LOVE
	HELP SOMEONE

In the Holy Bhagavad Gita, when Arjuna asks Lord Krishna the nature of a person who has risen above the Gunas, Lord Krishna says such a person acts neutral at all times and behaves with equanimity at all times.

समदुःखसुखः स्वस्थः समलोष्टाश्मकाञ्चनः ।
तुल्यप्रियाप्रियो धीरस्तुल्यनिन्दात्मसंस्तुतिः ॥ 24॥

Sama dukha sukha svasthaha sama loshtashma kaanchanaha
Thulya priya priyo dheera thulya nindhatma samsthutihi

मानापमानयोस्तुल्यस्तुल्यो मित्रारिपक्षयोः ।
सर्वारम्भपरित्यागी गुणातीतः स उच्यते ॥ 25॥

Maanapa maanayor thulyasthulyo mithraripakshayoho
Sarvarambha parityagi gunathithaha sa uchyathe

"Those who have equanimity in happiness and sorrow; who are established in the self; who look at the stone and a piece of gold with equal value; who remain the same amid pleasant and unpleasant events; who are intelligent; who accept both blame and praise with equanimity; who remain the same in honor and dishonor; who treat both friend and enemy alike; they are said to have risen above the 3 Guṇas."[12]

REFLECTION

There are 6 simple steps in this exercise.

1. Draw 3 boxes, one on top of the other, representing a 3-Step Ladder with the bottom being Tamas, the second being Rajas, and the top being Satva.
2. Within the bottom step, include your current qualities that exhibit Tamas during your day. For example, if you are experiencing procrastination, grief, confusion, depression, addictions, or lethargy, note it.
3. Next, for Rajas, include the feelings that emerge from your actions during your regular day. For example, note if you are experiencing anxiety, stress, worry, or fear.
4. Next, for Satva, include what you want to attain. For example, peace, happiness, joy, wisdom, and resilience.
5. Look at your ladder, and circle which Gunas you are experiencing the most in your day-to-day life. You can combine Tamas and Rajas, which is fine, or Rajas and Satva. The idea is to identify the most prominent Guna state in your day.

---

12   The Holy Bhagavad Gita 14:25-25

6. Next, write down which Guna you need to work on to move to Satva.

All the Gunas that we discussed above can influence our state of mind. Next, let's take a look at how this happens.

STATES OF MIND

"Focus and simplicity . . . once you get there, you can move mountains." - Steve Jobs

Have you ever found yourself struggling to focus during your day?

Focus is a very important attribute that is required not only to carry out our jobs at work but also to discipline our mind to move towards peace. It is one of the secret sauces behind success and happiness. It has been scientifically proven that focus enhances clarity in thinking, problem-solving, decision-making, productivity, and developing resilience.

We all have been granted the same 24 hours in a day. However, how do some people utilize it efficiently, while some others do not?

It is because they spend their focus, time, and energy very consciously and cautiously. In today's busy world surrounded by mobile phones, devices, gadgets, internet, and social media your attention is the first to be stolen with just the sound of a notification. Once your attention is grabbed, your time and energy move away from you.

Distractions have become part of our daily life, keeping us always busy and pulling us in different directions. There are external distractions in the form of phone calls, texts, or emails, and there are internal distractions in the form of our own thoughts, beliefs, memories, and imaginations. These distractions cause stress, anxiety, depression, and more mental health issues, leading to disappointments and diseases in our lives.

When we are distracted, our minds keep changing based on the fluctuations of the Gunas. When this happens, our minds switch between different states that determine our balance.

Based on Patanjali's *Yoga Sutras*, our mind has different states based on the agitations:

Kshipta (chaotic mind)—A chaotic mind is one that is always distracted and restless during the day as it is dominated by Rajas.

Muda (dull mind)—A dull mind is when you are dominated by Tamas and become lethargic and uninterested in carrying out any activity.

Vikshipta (partially focused mind)—In a partially focused state, you switch between Tamas and Rajas where you carry out work but you are also carried away by your distraction.

Ekagra (one-pointed mind)—In the one-pointed mind-state, your mind is in concentration. This is an ideal state to move to meditation. This is also the state where your energy is focused, enabling you to achieve your goals with peak efficiency. Satva Guna emerges from this state.

Niruddha (fully absorbed mind)—In Niruddha, the mind is in full control and is in equilibrium. It is also the state where the mind has merged with the activity or object at hand that allows our

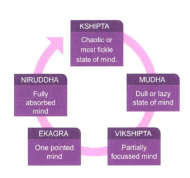

higher self to express itself in wholeness. Satva is the predominant Guna in this state.[13]

As you can see in the diagram above, kshipta and muda represent lower levels of our mind, and vikshipta, ekagra, and niruddha represent the higher levels of our mind.

You may have noticed that during your day, your mind may normally be in one of these states. When we are in a chaotic or lazy state of mind, we usually exhibit the Tamas Guna and have feelings of boredom, lethargy, procrastination, and disappointment. As you know, the dull mind is highly agitated and is in a state of no action or inertia. The thoughts that arise in this state are negative in nature and carry low energy. The same also applies when our mind is completely focused; we carry positive energy.

Our mind needs to be elevated to the ekagra state to utilize its highest potential. This is essential to carry out any kind of productive work in our lives, whether it is spiritual or material.

MANAGING DISTRACTIONS

1. **IDENTIFY**—Identify the external distractions around you that cause you distraction during your day. For example, it could be your physical environment, people, media, technology, etc.
2. **OBSERVE**—Observe your internal distractions that impact you during your day. For example, it could be your thoughts, feelings, beliefs, memories, etc.
3. **ASSESS**—Assess how you feel after getting distracted.
4. **REFLECT**—Reflect on what you would do if you were not distracted.

---

13   Patanjali, "Samadhi Pada."

According to the Holy Bhagavad Gita, the impurities of the mind subjected to different vasanas can be elevated to higher states only when we execute selfless actions that lead to a purified mental state, which reflects the higher possibilities within us. We all have the internal resources to elevate our minds from lower to higher forms. However, it does not happen automatically and requires effort from our end to move from each lower state to the higher and then to the highest.

Hence, it is important to develop a conscious mental discipline to move into higher levels of our mind.

For example, when you are in Tamas Guna and are experiencing grief, you are in kshipta or muda.

Performing at your highest efficiency in this state is complicated because your thoughts and emotions generate lower vibrational energy that may not produce the best results. So the mind, in a chaotic and dull state, needs to be moved to a partially focused state through carrying out actions that require focus, withdrawing yourself from distractions. Once the focus is improved and becomes one pointed, then it becomes capable of tapping into your innate wisdom through meditation. Our minds can perform at their best ability only if we are able to focus our attention. A disturbed mind can neither help us discover peace nor enable us to achieve our goals in life efficiently.

Next, we will look at how these Gunas influence our energy.

GUNAS, THOUGHTS, EMOTIONS, AND ENERGY

"The energy of the mind is the essence of life." - Aristotle

Many of us know that our mind, body, and spirit are strongly interconnected with each other, and we know how they influence each other in impacting our mental and physical health.

The strongest link that connects all these attributes of holistic health together is our energy. We all have a life force that runs through us, which makes us live. There are many names for it. Some may call it prana, chi, ki, etc. When this life force stops flowing, the body dies.

Everything in the universe is made of matter and energy. According to Unified Field Theorem, the entire 3,000-fold universe from the largest quasar to the smallest virus is composed in its actuality of a coherent energy field, which is only a component of the greater energy field of the universe. Unity of these is the unified coherent energy of the universe.

This theory also mentions that all matter and psychological functions in the form of thoughts, beliefs, emotions, and attitudes possess energy. The life force within us is made of 3 major elements. The 3 elements are auras, chakras, and meridians. We are all made of energy layers and energy fields that we carry with us wherever we go. This energy field is called our aura and includes 7 layers of our subtle bodies around us: ethereal, emotional, mental, astral, celestial, etheric template, and casual.

AURAS

The energy field that we all carry is called aura and is influenced by thoughts and emotions experienced by our minds. This is invisible to our eyes. However, we can experience this energy field based on the vibrations passed on to us. We may have experienced positive and negative vibrations by going to certain places or meeting certain people in our life. Highly positive or enlightened beings carry a powerful aura, and that is why when we meet or stay in their presence we feel highly energized and vice versa. The energy carried by our aura can also be impacted by being in certain places or interacting with certain people. Everything—places, devices, people, animals, and plants—have these energy fields. For example, many of us experience a sense of calm or peace while being at places of worship or in nature because of the positive vibrations carried by that place.

Many of us have heard the term *Karma* in our life. The Sanskrit meaning of Karma is action. Our actions determine our experiences in our world. We all perform actions based on our thoughts, beliefs, and emotions. The motive or the intent behind the action is what determines whether our action is good or bad. As discussed in the first chapter, our thoughts carry energy based on the intent behind it. We all know that every action has a result associated with it. According to the law of Karma, there is a cause and effect associated with it. Every time we perform an action based on our inner tendencies, our vasanas become stronger. Every result of action has a cause associated with it.

Any action that is performed with an ego attitude and selfish interest develops attachment and can leave residue or traces as footprints in our minds. If you hate someone, for example, thoughts of hatred pollute your mind and prompt you to carry actions of hatred towards the other person. Continuing this action not only leaves the traces for future action but also leaves the negative energy within us. Now, as we follow the same pattern, we keep building this up, which eventually leads to poisoning of ourselves by ourselves. Many of us believe that it is God punishing us. However, it is not God but our own actions that have caused us to reap the effects of our actions. So based on the law of cause and effect, whatever energy or thoughts you put out, you get the same back to yourself in the form of your experiences.

CHAKRAS

Our vasanas are stored in energy centers in our body called chakras. Even if we have forgotten about our past actions, the imprints are still there. The meaning of chakra in Sanskrit is "spinning wheel," and we all have 7 chakras in our body that are each connected to the functioning of an organ in our body. Each of these chakras are storehouses of our thoughts, emotions, and beliefs. Through this connection, based on the energy stored in the chakra, it can impact the functioning of a particular organ in our body. For example, a negative emotion of fear is associated with the root chakra and can lead to feelings of depression, insecurity, anxiety, excessive worrying, codependency, and feelings of loss.

The 7 chakras are:

1. Root—at the base of your spine
2. Sacral—just below the belly button
3. Solar plexus—the upper abdomen
4. Heart—center of the chest
5. Throat——center of the neck
6. Third eye—point between the eyebrows
7. Crown—at the top of the head

Various experiences throughout our day-to-day life can affect our chakras. The experiences in our lives and the emotions of fear, hatred, grief, love, and envy can impact our chakras. When our chakras are balanced and open, we experience harmony, grounding, self-expression, healthy communication, and healthy relationships. When they are blocked, they can spin slower, or they can sometimes completely stop spinning.

For example, an energy block in the solar plexus, which is associated with confidence, self-esteem, courage, trust, "gut feelings," action, vitality, and intention, can cause stomach issues, irritable bowel syndrome, adrenal issues, and a need for control.

Please use the below test to do a chakra assessment to find out if the chakras in your body are balanced or not. As you go through the assessment, mark your findings under the heading "My chakra is . . ." to help you take the necessary next steps.

CHAKRAS	UNDERACTIVE	OVERACTIVE
Crown Chakra	• Misunderstood • Can't have fun • Unaware of denying one's spiritual connection	• Addicted to spirituality • Craving attention • Needing to be popular
Third Eye Chakra	• Can be easily influenced • Confused about purpose • Self-doubt	• Lost • Worrying • Seen as living in a fantasy world • Spaced out
Throat Chakra	• Can't express oneself • Afraid to speak in public • Cannot express creativity • Timid • Dependent	• Speaks too much • Criticizes • Stubborn • Bores others
Heart Chakra	• Self-pitying • Fears rejection • Uncertain • Unloved • Needy	• Entitled • Jealous • Blames others
Solar Plexus	• Low self-esteem • Procrastinates • Apathetic	• Judgmental • Bullying • Critical
Sacral	• Guilty • Shy • Overthinks	• Needs power • Manipulative • Craving
Root Chakra	• Frustrated • Fearful	• Big ego • Bossy • Dominating • Greedy • Violent • Cunning

CHAKRAS	BALANCED	MY CHAKRA IS . . .
Crown Chakra	• Joy • Wisdom • Compassion	
Third Eye Chakra	• Intuitive • Knows purpose • Charismatic • Seen as wise	
Throat Chakra	• Speaks truth • Creative • Can express self	
Heart Chakra	• Loving • Empathetic • Contagiously positive	
Solar Plexus	• Confident • Calm • Solves problems • Has integrity • Respects self and others	
Sacral	• Friendly • Playful	
Root Chakra	• Grounded • Trustworthy • Poised • Independent	

Please use the list below to identify the specific chakra that would require healing based on the current health issue(s) that you are experiencing in your life.

CHAKRA	ASSOCIATED DISEASES
CROWN CHAKRA	Multiple personality syndrome, Nervous system disorders, Neurosis, Paralysis, Parkinson's disease, Psychosis, Right eye problem, Schizophrenia, Senile dementia, Tiredness, Tremor, Vomiting, Alzheimer's disease, Amnesia, Bone disorders, Cancers, Depression, Dizziness, Epilepsy, Fear, Headache, Immune system problem, Insomnia, Learning difficulties, Migraine, Multiple sclerosis
THIRD EYE CHAKRA	High blood pressure, Hormonal imbalance, Insomnia, Left eye problem, Farsightedness, Migraine, Nervousness, Nervous breakdowns, Scalp problems, Shortsightedness, Sinus problems, Sty, Tension, Tension headaches, Tiredness, Tremor, Visual effects, Vomiting, Allergies, Amnesia, Anxiety, Blood circulation to head, Blindness, Brain tumor, Cataracts, Cancers, Chronic tiredness, Crossed eyes, Deafness, Dizziness, Drugs, Dyslexia, ENT problem, Earache, Fainting spells, Glaucoma, Growth issues, Headaches

CHAKRA	ASSOCIATED DISEASES
THROAT CHAKRA	Sore throat, Stammer, Stiff neck, Teeth/Gum problem, Thyroid problem, Tinnitus, Tonsils, Excessive talking, Upper digestive tract problem, Vomiting, Whooping cough, Asthma, Bronchitis, Colds, Cough, Ear infections, Fear, Hearing problems, Hay fever, Hoarseness, Laryngitis, Lost voice, Mental confusion, Mouth ulcers, Pain in upper arm
HEART CHAKRA	Lung problem, Nail-biting, Pain in lower arms/hands, Pneumonia, Respiratory problem, Shortness of breath, Sleep disorders, Smoking, Tremor, Allergies, Asthma, Blood circulation problem, Breast cancer, Bronchitis, Chest congestion, Circulation problem, Cough, Fatigue, Heart diseases, High blood pressure, Hyperventilation, Immunity, Influenza
SOLAR PLEXUS	Gallstones, Heartburn, Hepatitis, Jaundice, Kidney problem, Decreased immunity, Liver problem, Pancreatitis, Peptic ulcer, Smoking, Stomach problem, Shingles, Ulcers, Vomiting, Abdominal cramps, Acidity, Anorexia, Bulimia, Chronic tiredness, Diabetes, Digestive problem, Eating disorder, Fear, Food allergies, Gastritis, Gallbladder problem

CHAKRA	ASSOCIATED DISEASES
SACRAL CHAKRA	Irritable bowel, Kidney problem, Menstrual problem, Muscle spasms, Ovarian cysts, Overeating, Premenstrual syndrome, Prostate disease, Stomach problem, Testicular disease, Uterine fibroids, Vomiting, Womb problem, Addiction to junk food, Alcohol, Backache, Bed-wetting, Bladder problem, Creative blocks, Cystitis, Fear, Fertility, Fibroids, Miscarriages, Frigidity, Hip problem, Impotence
ROOT CHAKRA	Money addiction, Migraine, Obesity, Pain at base of spine, Piles, Prostate cancer, Rectal cancer, Spine problem, Sciatica, Skin problem, Stomach problem, Swollen ankles, Weak legs, Weight problem, Addictions, Addictive behavior, Ankle problem, Anorexia, Backaches, Blood diseases, Bone problem, Cold feet, Constipation, Colitis, Depression, Diarrhea, Eczema, Frequent urination, Gambling, Glaucoma, Hemorrhoids, Hip problem, Hypertension, Impotence, Itching, Kidney stones, Knee problem, Leg cramps, Menstrual problem

Along with auras and chakras, another important energy element that we are composed of includes the meridians, which are the energy pathways to various parts of the body. The energy generated or carried from the chakras flows or is distributed through the meridians and nourishes our entire body.[14]

MERIDIANS

Meridians are energy paths that flow in our body that influence the functioning of organs. For example, the meridian associated with

---

14   "Diseases and Associated Chakras," Reiki Rays.

lungs, when blocked or affected, can impact the functioning of the lungs and can result in physical manifestation of lung diseases. There are 12 major meridians that run on each side of our body, and one side mirrors the other. Each meridian is correlated to an internal organ. Each organ has its own functions that may be physiological or invisible energy functions and highly depends on other organ systems. Energy and blood are constantly flowing through the meridians. The meridians communicate information to your organs, such as the need for temperature regulation, emotional regulation, and more. When your meridians and organs are in harmony, your body is more likely to be in a healthy condition. When you are experiencing stress, the meridians can become congested or blocked. This can have an effect on the mind-body-spirit connection.

For any appliance to function effectively, it needs to be connected to electricity. If there are any defects in the appliance, electricity cannot flow properly. Similarly, only when the life force in us is not blocked and flows properly can our body and mind work efficiently.

Any health issue initially originates in the energy body before it manifests as a physical disease. According to the system of Reiki, most of the physical and mental health issues we experience are due to imbalance in the energy flows within our own system. In essence, when we entertain negative thoughts, emotions, or beliefs, we are self-poisoning our own energy bodies with negative energy, eventually leading to our own degradation.

As we saw in the previous chapter, every thought generates an emotion. Every emotion has an intensity and generates emotional energy. Our energy level decreases when the intensity of negative feelings we experience increases. However, when the power of positive emotions we entertain increases, our energy level increases.

When we closely look at our energy levels during our day, we will notice that our emotional energy fluctuates based on the underlying layers of vasanas, Gunas, and mind-state and that there is a direct mapping between them as shown in the picture below.

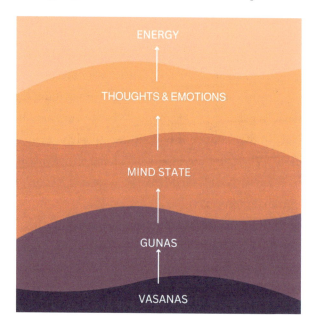

According to David R. Hawkins, the author of *The Map of Consciousness Explained,* we all have energy fields with a certain calibration level.

When we vibrate at an energy field of a frequency 200 Hz and above, we derive power and are in the positive zone, whereas when we vibrate at an energy field less than 200 Hz, we are in the negative zone and perceive the world through weakness, helplessness, and frustration.

Examples of some of the emotions described by David R. Hawkins that are less than 200 Hz at their calibration level include: shame (20), guilt (30), desire (125), grief (75), and anger (150).

Emotions that are above 200 Hz include: courage (200), love (500), joy (540), peace (600), and enlightenment (700–1000).

As you notice from the above examples, when you experience negative emotions, the energy field is lower, whereas positive feelings have higher energy.

Various research studies show that emotional energy, when stored, impacts the health of cells. Therefore, it is essential to shift and release emotional energy so that it does not block us from being in a balanced state of mind. As no emotion stays forever, we can use our feelings to guide us to areas that need attention and take action to shift them towards a higher and more positive energy level. Most of the time, we get caught up in our negative emotions and end up in a state where we cannot think clearly, make decisions, and perform at our best. It is only by organizing our energies and aligning to the divine energy that we can develop a conscious and improved quality of life. A simple way to regulate the emotional energy fluctuation is by observing our energy level and regulating our emotions.

EMOTION REGULATION

"Positive and negative emotions cannot occupy our minds at the same time." - Napoleon Hill

In life, we encounter different types of people and situations. Some people in our life help us learn and grow. Others drain our energy and suck us into a place of negativity. The negative energy, whether verbal or nonverbal, can impact our mindset and sometimes even paralyze us from moving forward in our life. The negative emotions caused by negative social interactions can make us feel lost and unhappy.

How do we regain our energy to move forward in our life?

One of the most effective ways to regain energy is by self-regulating our thoughts and emotions. By training our minds, we can elevate ourselves to a centered state that remains unaffected internally irrespective of our external situations.

The centered state is where we have self-control or control over our mind and use it effectively rather than it using us. Through this process, we will channel our energies in the right direction to help us achieve our goals, improve our focus and productivity, and live a peaceful and happy life.

Five simple steps to transform our negative emotions (SIFTE):

1. **Stop**—When a negative thought or emotion arises in your mind, stop for a moment before judging the feeling. For example, using simple breathing exercises is one of the best ways to develop the awareness needed to stop.

2. **Identify**—Identify the emotion that you are experiencing by giving it a name. This allows us to separate ourselves from the negative emotion and distance from it. For example, using funny names to distinguish each negative emotion will help us develop mindfulness around it.

3. **Feel**—Pay close attention to the area where you feel the negative emotion strongly, and give it your full attention. For example, scan your body to find where you strongly feel the negative emotion, and stay with it.

4. **Talk**—Talk to the emotion, and ask why it came up and what action can help transform it. For example, talk to the feeling with love and compassion to understand what it needs from you and how you can take action to help change it.

5. **Execute**—Do the positive action that came out of the response. This helps to shift your focus towards a positive step that will help you to regain your positive energy back in your life.

It is not possible to completely eradicate negativity from others. However, by carrying out the above steps, we can take adequate measures to regulate our thoughts and emotions to regain our positive energy back into our lives rather than allowing negative emotions to affect and paralyze us from moving forward.

REFLECTION

1. What state of mind do you mostly find yourself in?
   a. Fully absorbed
   b. Chaotic
   c. Partially focused
   d. Focused
   e. Dull
2. What are the Gunas that you have experienced corresponding to the state of your mind?
3. What is the mind-state that you would like to transition to that would make your day peaceful?

TOOLS FROM ANCIENT WISDOM THAT HELPED ME

Thousands of years back, great spiritual beings who were called Rishis discovered ancient wisdom–based tools during their highest state of meditation that elevate the mind to develop mental discipline and eventually lead to a place of self-control, allowing the mind to expand and discover a person's true potential and to lead a life of peace and happiness. There are various powerful tools and practices based on ancient wisdom that were created and discovered for this purpose. These tools and practices have immense power to elevate and expand our thinking in order to create mental discipline that eventually leads us to a place of self-control. These powerful tools can be used to overcome and prevent us from having to deal with anxiety, depression, and loneliness by managing our emotions and aligning our body and spirit to achieve holistic wellness. Integrating these tools into our daily life not only helps our mind to remain healthy but also helps us lead a life of peace and happiness. A combination of these ancient tools, when applied consistently in our daily lives, can help us:

- Become more self-aware
- Develop a positive mindset
- Develop intuition
- Develop self-control
- Increase our emotional intelligence
- Develop inner mental stability and resilience
- Enhance our mood regulation
- Improve our immunity
- Harmonize our relationships
- Enhance clarity and decision-making
- Improve our holistic wellness
- Align our body, mind, and spirit to tap into our infinite potential
- Reframe our thinking, actions, and behavior to become transformed human beings

Reframing can help a person to function at their highest potential, face life's challenges and problems more courageously, and eventually, lead us to discover peace.

There are numerous tools—including mantras, meditation, mindfulness exercises, Yoga, Reiki, and more—that are from ancient wisdom and can be used for daily purposes. Some of these tools like Yoga and Reiki should be learned from an expert or teacher in order to implement them. The simple tools mentioned below can be practiced by anyone regardless of age, religion, or culture.

MANTRAS

The entire universe is believed to have manifested from sound.

Many of us know that the sounds of nature have extraordinary healing powers and energy. Thousands of years ago, during the Vedic times, a divine language called Sanskrit was discovered from the sounds of nature. The meaning of the word *Sanskrit* is derived from "Sam" and "Krit," which together means "fully formed" or "fully constructed."

Sanskrit is believed to be the language of gods that was designed to align our body and mind to nurture and transform us to realize our true potential. Ancient scriptures that include the Vedas, Upanishads, the Holy Bhagavad Gita, Mahabharata, the Ramayana, and more were written in Sanskrit. Some of the secret techniques in the ancient scriptures were meditation, Yoga, and mindfulness.

According to Judith Tyberg, an American author and renowned Sanskrit scholar, "Every alphabet in Sanskrit has sound and power. This intrinsic power can always convey the sense that is inseparably related to the sound. In the sacred Sanskrit scriptures, this power was not only intuitively expressed but consciously wielded. And the power was not only of the human mind but of the spirit."[15]

The vocabulary of the Sanskrit language is so vast and rich that every word in Sanskrit has at least 32 meanings based on the context in which it is used. It is logical, unambiguous, and constructed based on syntactic rules.

The sounds of Sanskrit were formulated into powerful mantras with healing powers by ancient spiritual masters. The word *mantra* is derived from 2 Sanskrit words, "Man" and "Tra." Man means "mind," and Tra means "train." So the mantra means "one that trains your mind." These mind training tools, mantras, produce sounds that create powerful positive vibrations within a certain frequency level when chanted with the correct pronunciation.

Mantras help regulate our minds and bodies through the power of breath.[16]

The sounds in Sanskrit use different parts of our mouths and a certain level of breath and rhythm. For example, the first syllable अ (pronounced as Ah) requires a short breath, whereas the second syllable आ (pronounced as Aah), requires a long breath. So chanting mantras that include regulated inhalation and exhalation of breath not only helps regulate our breath but also our thoughts and our body.

There are 84 meridians on the roof of the tongue that are stimulated through the Sanskrit mantra, and scientific evidence shows that mantras can facilitate the release of secretions that strengthen our immune and neurological systems. Mantras stimulate the secretions of the pituitary gland and sends signals to the command centers of the brain—the hypothalamus and the pituitary and also to the pineal gland—which initiate a healing

---

15   Mishra, *The Wonder that is Sanskrit.*

16   Mishra, *The Wonder that is Sanskrit.*

response and send this response into the brain and throughout the body in the form of neurotransmitters and chemicals.

Mantras were designed to align and elevate our body, mind, and spirit to a higher level of consciousness. They provide the foundation for developing focus and memory apart from their healing powers, which are essential for a person to move towards meditation.

Each mantra has a specific purpose, meaning, and energy associated with it. Certain mantras are recommended to be chanted only during specific times of the day.

For example, Gayatri mantra is a mantra that protects the one who chants it, invokes their intelligence, and is supposed to be chanted during sunrise and sunset. Peace, or Shanti, mantras can be chanted at any time of the day and are designed to establish peace and harmony in the world. Similarly, healing mantras, like the Dhanvantari and Mrityunjay, help us heal from physical illness.

"Ohm" is considered the most simple and powerful mantra in the universe.

All sounds in nature are believed to have originated from Ohm'. Ohm constitutes 3 letters A - U - M with A (अ - pronounced as Ah) sound originating from the back of the throat, U (उ - pronounced as Oo) from the upper palate, and M ending in the lips (pronounced as im). Just chanting Ohm for a few minutes can provide profound physiological and psychological benefits in our lives. According to an article published in *Discover* magazine,[17] a vibrational frequency of 432 Hz is generated when you chant Ohm that is aligned to the frequency of nature. This produces alpha waves in our brain to create calmness. The article also shares the research results conducted by the *Indian Journal of Clinical Anatomy and Physiology* that states that when you chant

---

17   Sarkar, "Can Chanting OM Reduce Stress and Anxiety?"

Ohm the vibration from the ears passes through the vagus nerve and stimulates it to reduce various mental health and physical health issues including stress, anxiety, and depression. Chanting Ohm can help us purify our mind and body and develop mental clarity, focus, and memory. According to the renowned saint, the late Paramapujya Swami Jnanananda Saraswati (direct disciple of Swami Sivananda Maharaj), "One who chants Ohm regularly in the proper manner has the potential to attain ultimate realization of truth."

I have found it highly beneficial to chant mantras before beginning my meditation to help me focus to a state where my mind becomes quiet enough to carry out meditation. By allowing me to be present during chanting, it has also enabled me to develop mindfulness. Learning Sanskrit has helped me understand the meaning of mantras and chant them correctly to raise positive energy.

MANTRA MEDITATION

1. Sit in a comfortable position and close your eyes.
2. Chant "Ohm," focusing on the sound of the mantra every time you repeat it (21 times).
3. Keep your attention on the A(ah)-U(oo)-M(im) sounds, and notice vibrations in your head.
4. Feel the positive energy spread throughout your body.
5. Once you feel energized, slowly open your eyes.

As you continue this practice, your self-awareness, focus, and mindfulness will improve.

BREATHWORK

Different types of breath constitute our body. Breathwork is the most straightforward practice that can help us to settle our thoughts and emotions into a calm state.

Based on our thinking and emotions, our breathing pattern changes. When you practice regulated breathing, your thoughts and feelings eventually become regulated. Numerous breathing exercises have been prescribed in Yoga that can be carried out under the guidance of an expert teacher. Whatever the breathing exercise you choose, the idea lies in regulating the incoming and outgoing breath in a systemic rhythm. Pranayama, being the most popular breathwork with focus and total involvement, can help clear blockages of prana in different parts of our body, regulate oxygen within our body, improve blood circulation, help us develop mindfulness, and enable internal cleansing of mind and body equally. This is a simple and very powerful practice that can be done in less than 5 minutes to reset your energy during different emotional states of stress, anxiety, depression and more to calm your system and bring it back to a natural state of calmness so you can continue with positive energy.

SIMPLE BREATHING EXERCISE

1. Sit in a comfortable position.
2. Inhale a long deep breath while keeping your attention in your diaphragm or base of the chest.
3. Hold your breath as long as you can.
4. Exhale slowly, letting your breath out through your mouth, and notice the diaphragm muscles move outward.
5. Continue steps 2 through 5 as many times as possible.

MEDITATION

Meditation is a simple and powerful practice that can help purify our hearts, sharpen our intelligence, and help develop peace within us to face our daily challenges in life. I have found it effective to act as an internal guard to maintain calm when things don't work as planned. Meditation means giving love and attention to ourselves in order to tap the infinite potential of our minds. Meditation can help us to create inner peace and joy in order to prepare us to stay calm while we encounter the challenges of the day. I would like to give you an example of how meditation has helped me to remain calm and provided me clarity to accomplish a recent achievement in my life.

As a part of progressing in my career, I had to complete a certification. So I started my day with meditation and prepared myself for the day before heading out for my examination. When I reached the exam center, the examiner verified my details and tried to enter an authorization code to start the exam. However, the code did not work even after several attempts. Meditation helped me to remain calm, patient, and grounded. This allowed the examiner also to try alternatives and find a solution that helped to get a new code that worked. Although I started my exam 15 minutes late, I was able to remain calm, think clearly, and focus on my responses. That helped me to provide accurate answers and accomplish my certification successfully.

Changing our thinking patterns takes time, effort, practice, and commitment. These tools have been integrated into various modalities, including coaching and therapy, to enable quick personal transformation. These modalities can tap into our subconscious mind by using ancient wisdom–based tools and techniques to reprogram our thinking patterns and behavior.

We often practice these tools independently but must remember to integrate them into our relationships, work, family, etc. Transformation will not happen if we practice and don't integrate these techniques into various situations in our life. For the tools to work at their best, we should be ready to let go of our old patterns and behaviors and be open to change. Taking a few minutes of our day to integrate daily spiritual practices to train our minds and connect with a higher energy source helps us develop positivity, mindfulness, and inner stability that improve our emotional wellness and lead us to become self-resilient in our lives.

As we choose a variety of daily activities that include daily walks and exercise to assist in physical wellness, it is essential to train and balance our minds with the assistance of ancient wisdom–based spiritual tools for our overall well-being.

Training our minds is not a one-day affair. It may take days, months, or several years to get to a place of self-control based on the level of the constitution of our minds and bodies.

As these tools are not for religious purposes, they can be applied by anyone who has learned them through proper guidance. These tools do not have side effects and are meant to train the mind to create mental discipline.

One important thing to note here is that these tools will not make magic happen outside you but will bring transformation within you when you integrate them into your daily life, as long as you have an open attitude, humility, trust, sincerity, commitment, and readiness to change.

उद्धरेदात्मनाऽऽत्मानं नात्मानमवसादयेत्।
आत्मैव ह्यात्मनो बन्धुरात्मैव रिपुरात्मनः।।6.5।।11

Udhareth aatmana aatmanam na aatmanam avasadayeth
Aatmaiva aatmano banduratmaiva ripuratmanaha

"You have to uplift yourself and not allow your mind to sink because your mind itself is your friend and enemy."

Next, let's look at the perspective from the Holy Bhagavad Gita on developing stability of mind and resilience.

BECOMING UNSHAKEABLE

Prince Arjuna was a great warrior. He was talented, brilliant, mighty, and skilled in various weapons, including archery. However, when he had to fight the Mahabharata war against his own cousins, uncles, and teachers to protect his kingdom, he became filled with self-doubt.

When self-doubt struck Arjuna, he went through a myriad of physical and mental sensations that prompted him to run away from his duty to fight the war. He lost his confidence and was filled with grief and disappointment. To escape the war, he tried to convince Lord Krishna, who was his charioteer and his coach, that fighting the war would lead to killing his own people and incurring sin in the future.

In our lives, we also enter states of self-doubt when we face challenging situations or problems with our family, friends, and peers at our workplaces. Confusion, fear, and anxiety crop up, making us incapable of thinking clearly and finding the best solution to our problems.

Arjuna was not incapable or did not lack knowledge or skills. His attachment towards his own people was the obstruction that prevented him from acting as his true self and executing his dharma as a warrior. The teachers, uncles, and relatives who Arjuna was attached to did not have the same attachment back to him and joined the opposition army of his cousins. Arjuna knew that his cousins had harmed him and his family all throughout their life. He also knew that letting them rule the kingdom would mean letting injustice prevail in the world.

In spite of knowing all this, the questions that Arjuna confronted were: What if I incur sin by killing them? What will happen to their family if they die? Is it not better to not fight the war?

Many of us also get into this cycle of overthinking, worry, and anxiety where we become stuck and helpless in our own thoughts. This vicious cycle takes away our peace of mind and makes us live in disappointment.[18]

Arjuna's emotions overpowered his rational thinking and discriminative power, which made him feel helpless and not prepared for fighting the war. He understood that he would not be able to fight the war with this unbalanced emotional state.

Seeing Arjuna's desperate emotional condition, Lord Krishna tells him to get rid of the emotional weakness and rise up from this state of mind.

क्लैब्यं मा स्म गमः पार्थ नैतत्त्वय्युपपद्यते ।
क्षुद्रं हृदयदौर्बल्यं त्यक्त्वोत्तिष्ठ परन्तप ॥ ३॥

Klaibhyam ma sma gamaha partha nai-tatva-yupapadhyate Kshudram Hrudaya Dourbalyam Tyakta uthishta parantapa

"This unmanliness does not suit you, Partha. Let go of the weakness of your heart and arise."

However, as Arjuna is in a feeble mindset, he continues to ask questions of Lord Krishna on how he can fight against his own

---

18   The Holy Bhagavad Gita 6:5

teachers, uncles, and noble people who are standing against him on the enemy front when he does not know who will win the war.

Arjuna, who is stuck, helpless, confused, and sorrowful, realizes that he is unable to uplift himself without further guidance from Lord Krishna and surrenders at the feet of the Lord and requests him to show him the way out.

कार्पण्यदोषोपहतस्वभावः
पृच्छामि त्वां धर्मसम्मूढचेताः ।

Kaarpanyadosho upahatha svabhavaha
Prachami tvaam dharma samooda chetaha

"I am confused, and my nature is overpowered by anxiety."

यच्छ्रेयः स्यान्निश्चितं ब्रूहि तन्मे
शिष्यस्तेऽहं शाधि मां त्वां प्रपन्नम् ॥ 7॥

Yat shreyaha syath nishchitham broohi tanme
Shishyas the aham shaadhi maam tvam prapannam

"Please tell me what is the best. I am your student and surrender before you, my Lord."[19]

We all come across similar situations in our life when we are stuck don't know how to move forward. When I encountered those moments, I approached my spiritual mentors, coaches, and teachers who showed me the right direction to discover the next big step to take in my life. I knew that they had the expertise and experience, so I trusted them to help me bring change in my life.

19   The Holy Bhagavad Gita 2:7

My coaches and mentors revealed the blind spots within me that were causing me emotional pain and discomfort. They guided me by questioning my beliefs and returning my peaceful mindset.

It was not just one but many who walked with me along the way to show me the light, and I am grateful to have been fortunate to connect with them in my life. Personal development is a process and does not happen in a day, but when you have the earnest desire to change and associate with great and wise people, internal transformation will happen over time. It is indeed true that when the student is ready, the teacher appears.

It is when Arjuna becomes ready to listen to guidance that Krishna begins sharing with Arjuna that it is not worthwhile to grieve over things that are out of his control. As Krishna continues to share about the impermanence of life, he mentions to Arjuna that as a warrior, his duty is to fight the war for justice. If he fails to do so, then he will incur the results of the wrong deed and would need to face disrespect, humiliation, and defamation from people around him for running away from the war.

Krishna then tells Arjuna to wake up and perform his duty regardless of the results of the war. When you work with such an attitude, not concerned about the results but with full focus on it, you do not have to face the bondage of Karma. It is only with a one-pointed mind that someone can achieve success in their life where the heart and intellect work together in perfect harmony. Working with such a state of mind will cleanse the impurities of the vasanas accumulated in us and purify our minds.

Krishna mentions the state of mind that is in perfect equilibrium and calls those people who have attained it "the steady-minded" and "wise ones." The steady-minded are not affected by success or failure, happiness or sorrow, and are free from suffering.

As soon as Arjuna hears this statement, he becomes curious to know more and asks Lord Krishna to describe the specialty of the steady-minded people.

स्थितप्रज्ञस्य का भाषा समाधिस्थस्य केशव ।
स्थितधी: किं प्रभाषेत किमासीत व्रजेत किम् ॥ 54॥

Sthitha prajnasya kaa bhasha samadhistasya keshava
Sthithadhihi kim prabhasheth kimaseeth vrajeth kim

"What are the characteristics of a man of steady wisdom?
How do they walk, talk, and sit?"

Lord Krishna calls this unshakeable person "Sthitaprajna"—meaning "steady wisdom"—the one who has attained an emotionally stable and resilient mindset that does not waver with failures, criticisms, or challenges. Anyone in this world, regardless of religion, can become Sthitaprajna if they follow specific mental disciplines crucial to mastering the mind.

Lord Krishna provides his response as:

श्रीभगवानुवाच ।
प्रजहाति यदा कामान्सर्वान्पार्थ मनोगतान् ।
आत्मन्येवात्मना तुष्ट: स्थितप्रज्ञस्तदोच्यते ॥ 55॥

Prajahaathi yada kaaman sarvan partha manogathaan
Aatmanyeva aatmana thushtaha sthithaprajna tadochyathe

"The one who has won over the selfish desires of the mind and is content in himself with a purified mind is said to have achieved the steady mindset of a Sthitaprajna."

दुःखेष्वनुद्विग्रमनाः सुखेषु विगतस्पृहः ।
वीतरागभयक्रोधः स्थितधीर्मुनिरुच्यते ।56।

Dukheshvanu dvignamanaha sukheshu vigata sprahaha
Veetha raga bhaya krodhaha sthitha dheer muniruchyathe

"The mind that is undisturbed in pain and pleasure, free from attachment, fear, and anger is said to have steady wisdom."

यः सर्वत्रानभिस्नेहस्तत्तत्प्राप्य शुभाशुभम् ।
नाभिनन्दति न द्वेष्टि तस्य प्रज्ञा प्रतिष्ठिता ॥ 57॥

Yaha sarvatraanabhi sneha tat prapya shubhashubham
Naabhi nindathi na dveshti tasya prajna prathishtitha

"One who is unattached in all conditions, good and evil, and responds to criticism or praise is said to have perfect knowledge."

यदा संहरते चायं कूर्मोऽङ्गानीव सर्वशः ।
इन्द्रियाणीन्द्रियार्थेभ्यस्तस्य प्रज्ञा प्रतिष्ठिता ॥ 58॥

Yada samharathe chaayam koormo anganiva sarvashaha
Indriyaani indriyarthebhyas thasya prajna prathishtitha

"One who is able to withdraw the senses from their objects, just as a tortoise withdraws its limbs into its shell, is established in divine wisdom."

The secret to success of many great leaders, visionaries, musicians, athletes, and artists who have gone above and beyond their mental limitations to create magic in this world lies in the development of the resilient mindset also known as Sthithaprajna.

The ancient wisdom techniques and guidance offered by Lord Krishna to train the mind eventually enabled Arjuna also to rise to the state of Sthithaprajna and carry out his dharma as a prince that brought Arjuna and his brothers, called "Pandavas" (sons of King Pandu), together in victory in the Mahabharata war.

Next, let's look at some of the qualities and paths that one can take to become a Sthitaprajna and become resilient.[20]

ETHICS

Have you heard of the popular quote from Billy Graham that goes:

"When wealth is lost, nothing is lost; when health is lost, something is lost; when character is lost, all is lost"?

In a world where we live for survival based on food, money, and shelter, an essential element gradually diminishing from within us is ethics. Ethics is a word that is derived from the Greek word *ethikos*, which refers to the moral principles that govern our character. A man without ethics is a man without character. Ethics are the moral values that build the foundation for becoming a true human.

However, from early childhood, we are raised to pay attention to ensure we have everything outside us that will keep us safe and secure and eventually lead us to happiness. In the urge to fulfill

---

20　The Holy Bhagavad Gita 2: 54-58

those needs, we run after one thing and another, be it fame, wealth, jobs, people, and more. When we focus on gaining these things in our life, many of us compromise our ethics, believing that nobody will find this out other than ourselves. As it is required to have fertile soil to grow beautiful plants, when our minds become fertile with positive values, it causes the seeds of wisdom within us to flourish.

We derive our values based on the principles we believe in our life. These values then become the pillars that hold together our identity. When we lose our value, we lose our identity. We derive our values from our past experiences that include upbringing and learning from our environment around us. Even if we have derived values that have not served us, we can change them anytime in our life.

Your values determine what is important for you in your life and influence your thoughts, attitude, actions, and decisions.

TYPES OF VALUES

Values are categorized into intrinsic and extrinsic.

Intrinsic values refer to values that are naturally in us that motivate us to grow and help us feel fulfilled. These values are not dependent on our external surroundings. They could include creativity, determination, perseverance, honesty, integrity, and more.

Extrinsic values refer to values that are dependent on external factors in order to satisfy our needs for approval or recognition. These include job security, social status, wealth, etc. Positive values make us behave as humans and help us build the power of resilience to face various stressful situations in our life. Our values make us who we truly are and determine the decisions we make in our life.

When you look at the great leaders in the world—Mahatma Gandhi, Abraham Lincoln, Winston Churchill, Nelson Mandela, Martin Luther King Jr., and many more—they all stood by their strong values and principles. Their values were the basis of their mindset that made up their character and gave them power to achieve great things in life.

Your values are your weapons to use when an adverse situation or difficult person appears in your life. The values that have enabled me to develop resilience are determination, perseverance, willpower, faith in God, humility, and kindness.

Perseverance has been a very powerful value that has always helped me to face failures and rise above them to continue towards my goals. When you know your values and act accordingly, you develop power to discriminate, which in turn helps you to distinguish right and wrong, leading to clarity. Values are your compass to help you move in the right direction in life.

For example, in your relationships you might value trust, respect, and support, whereas your spouse could have a similar or separate set of values that determine the strength of your relationship. Similarly, in your workplace you and your company have values. The alignment between your values and your company's values impacts your productivity, performance, and job satisfaction.

The more we live by our values the less will be our stress levels in life.

In the Holy Bhagavad Gita, Lord Krishna mentions the distinction between divine and demonic values, or qualities, that determines the success and failure of an individual as described below.

Lord Krishna states that the 3 demonic qualities are desire, anger, and greed.

When an individual leads a life with demonic qualities, they live at a lower level, which results in an impurified mind that causes harm to themselves and others.

The lower qualities in these individuals make them believe that the ultimate purpose of life is to become rich and satisfy all their desires, which makes them lead a life of ego, ignorance, arrogance, and hypocrisy. Living an unconscious life without faith and values will not bring happiness or success.

Therefore, the essential values to cultivate are explained in the shloka below.

अभयं सत्त्वसंशुद्धिर्ज्ञानयोगव्यवस्थितिः ।
दानं दमश्च यज्ञश्च स्वाध्यायस्तप आर्जवम् ॥ 1॥

Abhayam satva samshudhir guyana yogavyavasthihi
Dhaanam damashcha yagyashcha svadhyaya tapa aarjavam

अहिंसा सत्यमक्रोधस्त्यागः शान्तिरपैशुनम् ।
दया भूतेष्वलोलुप्त्वं मार्दवं हीरचापलम् ॥ 2॥

Ahimsa satyam akrodha thyagaha shanthir paishunam
Daya bhootheshvaloluptvam maardavam hrir acha palam

तेजः क्षमा धृतिः शौचमद्रोहोनातिमानिता ।
भवन्ति सम्पदं दैवीमभिजातस्य भारत ॥ 3॥

Thejaha kshama dhrithihi shoucham drohonathimanitha
Bhavanthi sampadam daivim abhijaathasya bharatha

"Oh Arjuna—referred to as Bharata here—the noble virtues of one with divine or godly qualities are fearlessness, purity of mind, steadfastness in spiritual knowledge, charity, control of the senses, sacrifice, study of the sacred books, penance, and straightforwardness; nonviolence, truthfulness, absence of anger, renunciation, peacefulness, restraint from fault-finding, compassion towards all living beings, absence of greed, kindness, modesty, steadiness; energy, forgiveness, courage in adversity, cleanliness, bearing enmity towards none, and absence of pride."

When one practices all of the above, the mind becomes prepared to elevate to a state of resiliency and efficiency.[21]

REFLECTION

Here are some questions to assist you in the process of reflecting on and identifying your values.

1. What are the values that you exhibit in your daily life?
2. What are the values that make you different from others around you?
3. What are the values that you have learned from your parents, teachers, friends, and coworkers?
4. What are the values that you exhibit in relationships at home and work?

DIFFERENT PATHS

Life is a journey, and we are all travelers who have unique paths. Although our paths may be different, we can make our journey a happy and enjoyable experience.

---

21   The Holy Bhagavad Gita 16:1-3

According to the Holy Bhagavad Gita, these paths are based on our intelligence, actions, and emotions. Since we are all different, we may all choose different paths to arrive at the abode of inner peace.

In the book *Self-Unfoldment* written by Swami Chinmayananda, the 4 types of personalities based on one's path are described below:

1. **Intellectual**—The intellectuals understand the world through logical thinking and are less emotional. They are driven by scientific evidence, facts, and reasoning and are suggested to follow the path of Jnana Yoga or knowledge.

2. **Emotional**—These are personality types who are driven by the heart. For such individuals, devotion is the prescribed method suggested in the Bhakti Yoga to attain peace.

3. **Action-oriented**—Individuals driven by actions believe in taking action and can't stop working. The prescribed method recommended in Karma Yoga of the Holy Bhagavad Gita is to perform selfless actions to exhaust the vasanas that cause desire and cloud thinking and emotions.

4. **General**—To a regular person who has average intellectual and emotional characteristics, the prescribed method is Hatha Yoga where the body is trained through postures and breathing exercises, like Pranayama, to develop discipline and attain peace.

An integration of all these types needs to be developed to bring about a balance in us. I have found in real life that a combination of these paths—intellectual, emotional, action-oriented, and general—have been helpful to me.

EMOTIONAL

In today's world, where development of the heart is diminishing, incorporating devotion can help with heart development. Faith and surrender are core to devotion.

Devotion is deep love that inspires you to go beyond your limitations and attain self-mastery. Devotion towards the higher power called God is called Bhakti in Sanskrit. Devotion can also be towards our passion or any work we do with deep love. Whatever the type of devotion we pursue, if our devotion allows us to move out from egocentric self and merge with the object of devotion, the devotee is elevated to a higher level of consciousness. This opens the flow of grace into our lives.

Devotion is essential to experience the power of grace that makes unimaginable miracles happen in our life. Prayer with devotion invokes grace when our ego surrenders to the higher power called by different names as God.

Devotion has helped me to understand the value of surrender and enabled me to stay grounded. Without faith, mere chanting of mantras or reading scriptures will not allow the heart to expand. Devotion can give rise to values of empathy, compassion, love, and forgiveness in us and towards other human beings. It also helps us to get out of the clutches of ego and detach ourselves. Devotion can be cultivated to a certain extent through music, dance, and other art forms.

ACTION

Another path that has been very helpful in reducing the agitations of my mind is performing selfless actions without being concerned about the results of the activity at hand. I have noticed that when we carry out any task in our day with such an attitude, there is less agitation within the mind as there is no anxiety or worry about the future results. Having complete involvement with love and deep focus on the task, creates an internal contentment, and the results thereby take care of themselves. This leads to inner freedom while doing our work, and work can become a joyful experience.

INTELLECTUAL

The intellectual personality type refers to those who prefer learning, understanding, and applying logic and reasoning without believing blindly or following superstitious beliefs. This involves having the right understanding based on evidence without arriving at conclusions based on assumptions. This is called *viveka*, which means "discrimination" or wisdom based on right thinking and perception of the external world around us. One of the ways to develop intellectual ability is through self-inquiry and asking the right questions. I have found that the more we ask questions to ourselves as a means to understand and improve ourselves rather than as self-criticism, the more we will be able to find answers from within. For example, if someone in your workplace begins to argue with you, you can use your discriminative power to not react and become emotionally involved with the argument but rather detach yourself and use your intelligence to guide you to think, communicate, and act appropriately. I have found this approach of using *viveka* very effective to handle conflicts at home and in the workplace.

GENERAL

Hatha Yoga for the general personality type brings about an alignment or balance between the mind, body, and spirit through regulating the breath. Our body and mind are so interlinked that we can use each for our holistic wellness. Hatha Yoga is considered to have various benefits for strengthening the body and the mind, reducing stress, and improving our mental and physical health.

The path of Hatha Yoga prescribed can bring balance to one's mind and body to work together so that the mind can enter a balanced state, which is essential to go into deeper modes of meditation. Unlike other ancient wisdom–based tools mentioned earlier, Yoga is recommended to be learned from an expert or a trained Yoga instructor before you integrate it into your daily practice.

These paths can be followed by anyone regardless of any religion one may belong to because these are meant to help the practitioner advance their body and mind to a place that becomes fit to realize inner peace and strength.

REFLECTION

1. Which path among the 4 matches your personality? (Intellectual, emotional, action-oriented, or general?)
2. Which among the 4 could lead you to a peaceful and resilient life?
3. What are the current obstacles in your life that are preventing you from becoming unshakeable or Sthitaprajna?

FOUR PILLARS TO PEACE

The journey to discovering inner peace is different for everyone based on their life experiences.

Integrating all the ancient wisdom–based tools that I have shared in the previous chapter over many years led me to train my mind for discovering my purpose in life and peace of mind.

In this section, I will share with you the 4 key pillars that have transformed me in my journey of life.

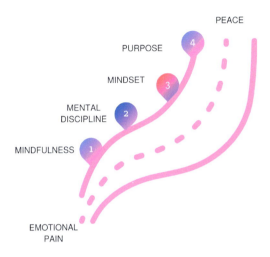

PILLAR ONE - MINDFULNESS

Mindfulness is an act of living in the present moment. This means being mindful of every moment in your life, paying complete attention, and not getting caught up in your past or future. Mindfulness can be practiced anytime and anywhere. Mindfulness helps me stay focused on my present moment. This activity not only helps to train our minds to improve our focus but also helps us to observe and respond to situations around us rather than reacting spontaneously. I practice it daily and have seen the profound benefits of protecting myself from negative experiences 90% of the time.

I apply mindfulness strategies when communicating with my family and coworkers. This has helped me to construct responses appropriately depending on the situation without getting into a conflict. I have implemented this into my life by being present and focusing on myself today and looking at each person I interact with as they are now without bringing in the past or judgments. This has allowed me to look at people and situations with gratitude.

Let me share an example of how I applied a simple practice in my parenting adventure with my daughter when she was two years old.

Every morning, we had an alarm without a snooze button that used to ring continuously. Did you guess who it was? Yes, it was that loud shrieking voice from a tiny body that sometimes annoys parents and makes them go crazy.

We had tried multiple ways to snooze this alarm, but nothing succeeded. So one day, I decided to talk to my daughter. I took a deep breath and sat next to her while she was dedicatedly doing her routine job of crying. I detached myself from her with no emotions and asked her why she was crying. She stopped crying for a few seconds and said, "Because I want to CRYYYYY!" I just nodded my head and took a breath again. A wonderful idea struck me. I asked her if she was willing to play a challenge with me until Easter, and she agreed.

I told her the rules of the challenge. Every morning when she woke up, she would blow air into an imaginary balloon and pop it when she felt like crying, and she would be rewarded with a prize if she won the challenge. She agreed as she loved balloons. The next day, as I had got so habituated listening to our house alarm that woke us up, I waited for the alarm, but to my surprise I saw that my daughter woke up quietly with a beautiful smile. Little did I imagine that this simple exercise would dramatically change my mornings.

By developing and inculcating these powerful practices into our daily life, we can create mental hygiene that develops our internal environment and prevents the external environment from affecting us.

PILLAR TWO - MENTAL DISCIPLINE

A mental discipline is one where you are in control of your mind rather than the mind being in control of you. It is one of the most essential factors required to achieve success in life. Like following a discipline in life brings an order, developing mental discipline will help us gain enormous strength, willpower, and energy throughout our day.

Numerous research studies have found that we entertain at least 50,000 thoughts per day. When we begin following every thought that arises in our mind, we become slaves of our mind that jumps from one thought to another according to its own whims and fancies.

Our mind, as mentioned in Chapter 3, is an instrument or vehicle that has been provided to us to help us move towards self-actualization to live at our best potential. However, like an instrument that needs to be learned and tuned to play it beautifully, if we do not tune and train our mind, it will act in the silliest ways possible. Let's imagine you are being taken to 2 classrooms in a school to pick the class you want to send your child to for learning. Classroom A has mischievous students running around, throwing things at each other, and talking while the teacher is teaching the class. Classroom B has disciplined students who are listening to the teacher attentively and taking down notes.

Which classroom would you pick?

As a parent, the environment of Classroom B is more conducive to learning and development. So if the teacher does not bring order to the class, the classroom will be noisy and disruptive, causing trouble not only to those who are in the class but also outside.

Let me share an example with you here of one such naughty student. As a part of pursuing my passion in music, I teach a group of students vocal music and veena on the weekends. One day, a five-year-old student named "Mike" joined the group of well-behaved and disciplined students. Mike was plump and looked very calm on the outside. I took him in and began teaching the lessons. The first few weeks went fine. However, after a few weeks as he became comfortable with the environment, the playfulness in Mike began showing up as walking on 4 legs, lying down on the floor, complaining about his day, distracting others, and losing focus on the lesson being taught. Other students in the class began to feel frustrated as they were eager to learn and found this behavior difficult to adapt to. As I watched this behavior, I initially told Mike to focus on his book and sing. He would listen but fall back into the old pattern again. It was funny to watch, but at the same time, it was not helping him learn.

So I told Mike, "Let's have someone team up with you." As Mike began teaming up with another student, he began watching and following the person on his team. This worked for a few minutes, but he would lose focus again. When I noticed this, I told Mike, "OK, let's play a game where you will get points for singing and lose points when you behave badly." He was up for it. I started marking points, and as he watched them go below 0, he looked concerned. Slowly, he sat erect and began singing with proper attention.

I did not have to say anything afterward because he took it as his responsibility to earn points and stand up for his team. Mike was in need of help and a little guidance in order to change his attitude in the class. Similarly, our minds also need to be trained to develop a mental discipline. This order depends on our priorities and intentions. One of the effective ways that enabled me to establish a mental discipline was developing a consistent routine for my day. The consistent routine includes activities where I spend my time, attention, and energy based on the value they add to my life. As I began developing discipline and added discrimination into the mix, my thoughts and emotions also began to follow an order.

When a thought arises in our mind, before jumping into action, it is important to think before we act. Most of us get into trouble when we become unconscious and follow our thoughts immediately. So developing awareness of our own thoughts and actions can help us become conscious. Once we have developed awareness, it is important to watch our thoughts as a policeman would watch every person on the street to find out if there is a hidden culprit. This requires us to develop alertness to help us discriminate between right and wrong. When we are in such a state, by monitoring every thought that pops into our mind, we can choose to act or not based on our discrimination.

Performing our actions in such a manner will cultivate mental discipline where we allow only what is necessary to be consumed and move towards a state of equilibrium that is the center of balance, equanimity, and peace.

In order to achieve the state of mental clarity, peace, stability, and freedom, it is important to train the mind in a positive direction as we would train a pet. All that comes into our mind need not necessarily be true and have to be believed. Before you believe the thoughts and emotions, check in with yourself and determine the validity of the thoughts or emotions, and then execute your actions. Take charge of your feelings before they take charge over you. It is your birthright to be happy and peaceful. You were born strong and peaceful. All is required for you to return your mind to its home, which is a state of peace.

As a trained gymnast can balance on a beam by using continued focus, practice, and by polishing their skills, we can all develop the balance within us that leads to a calm and peaceful state of mind. This balanced mind is a powerhouse that, when used intelligently, can do wonders in the world.

You can design your day the way you want when you have a powerful discipline. This includes investing your time and energy in yourself first before you invest in others.

I have found that cultivating a positive mindset in the morning and then refilling it with more positive habits has enabled me to sustain positivity throughout the day. Use your time and energy very carefully on people and activities.

PILLAR 3 - POSITIVE MINDSET

Do you know we all live in 2 worlds?

This might sound a bit strange, but we all carry an internal world within us and interact with the external world around us.

The internal world represents our mindset that processes the data from the external world and prompts us to take actions leading to our behaviors. It is made of our beliefs, thoughts, and attitudes that we use to perceive and respond to different situations that we face in our lives. This central processing unit determines our happiness or sorrow, success or failure in life based on its constitution.

The external world represents surroundings, people, and situations in our lives. Triggers from the external environment influence our internal environment through words or actions from those around us. These triggers, when not processed properly by our internal environment which is our mindset, lead us to unfavorable responses. As the external environment is always changing, it is not something that we can control. However, our internal environment within us can be changed and transformed based on the way we process the triggers from the external world. We receive information from our external environment, process it using our mindset, and then react or respond back to our external environment. Your emotional wellness, peace, and happiness are based on your internal environment and not your external environment.

I discovered the 5 P Model to develop a positive mindset, and it includes the stages below:

1. **PURIFY**

   This stage refers to purifying your mind before you set out to interact with anyone in your day. I use the SIFTE process discussed earlier in this chapter to cleanse my mind before I begin my day. This powerful exercise requires only 5 minutes and has allowed me to start with a clean state of mind.

2. **PREPARE**

   The preparation stage is to prepare your mind for the day. A simple way to prepare is to use your favorite meditation and anchor to a goal. By goal I don't mean to start thinking about your to-do list of unfinished tasks. What I mean is setting a goal about how you want to feel at the end of your day. For example, the goal that I set to have a peaceful day is saying to myself, "Whatever happens today, I will be happy and peaceful." You can also include a set of other positive affirmations to prepare yourself for your day.

3. **PRESENCE**

   Once you have purified and prepared yourself, it is important to move forward into your day with presence of mind in all possible interactions with people and situations as much as possible. It may be difficult when you begin this practice to always be present, but even if you fail, as you continue this practice, you will be able to master it and respond effectively. This is the stage to incorporate mindfulness as much as possible into everything in and around you. For example, be mindful during action and inaction, like being mindful of every bite of food that you eat, being mindful of the words that you speak, or being mindful of your thoughts when you are sitting idle.

4. **PERSPECTIVE**

   Perspective refers to the way you look at people and situations in your life. As in the previous step, once you have set the goal to be peaceful, it is essential for you to develop a positive perspective to achieve it. So whatever situation appears before you, translate it into a positive perspective in favor of your peace. This does not mean you have to keep quiet about a cruel action that someone does to you. This means responding in such a way that your internal peace remains unshattered. You can imagine it like a precious gift in your heart that you are protecting from others who want to steal it away from you. For example, the stealing could be in the form of negative criticism, blame, or anything that disturbs your peace. In order to carry out this perspective, you need to process your thoughts as soon as they emerge properly by asking a question like: How should I respond so that I can continue to be peaceful?

5. **PROVIDE**

When you have peace, you can provide peace to others also. When you are positive, you can offer positivity to others, too. So illuminate your environment with peace and positivity. Help someone without expecting anything in return and see how it makes you feel happier within. It does not have to be a hard task. It can be as simple as opening the door for someone.

As you continue taking these actions, you are not just helping others but you are helping yourself by enhancing positivity within you.

Let me share a personal example of the power of a positive mindset. I had recently registered to perform for a cultural event. Just 2 days before the performance, I received a call from the organizing committee saying they could not accommodate my performance. I listened to the person without judgment and responded with a thank-you. However, I remained optimistic, believing this had happened for a good reason and that a brighter opportunity awaited me. This positive thought brought in a surprise 2 days later as an invitation from a different organization who requested me to perform for their inauguration event. I felt pleased and delivered my vocal performance, which was more highly recognized and appreciated than I had imagined.

You can develop a positive mindset by shifting the way you look at every situation or person in your life positively even during the worst circumstances.

PILLAR 4 - PURPOSE

Have you ever lost direction in your life?

While planning a trip to a destination, we all prepare ourselves to understand the directions to the destination. We know that when we do not have a direction, we will become lost.

Similarly, our life is also a journey that could take us to the destination of happiness and peace. In order to get to our destination, we need to know the direction to go in. There could be many paths that we could follow to get to the destination. However, if we do not determine the right path, we end up getting lost.

Life is an opportunity whether we believe it or not. We have one chance in this world to live our beautiful life. With this one chance, we go through a myriad of events and get carried away living the life of others through the different relationships around us, pleasing everyone around us and believing these actions will take us to a place of happiness. Eventually, after going through the cycle of being born, receiving an education, getting married, having children, taking care of our family, going to work, and retiring some of us slowly start thinking about our life deeply.

Is there more to life? Why do we feel dissatisfied in spite of attending to our family, children, and jobs? What is the missing factor that we hardly pay attention to within us?

Many years back, I was in this place where I had everything around me but still felt that I had lost my direction and was living an empty life. I was living a basic life of eating, working, and sleeping. I had everything that life could offer me in the form of a good family, wealth, and health, but still there was something more that I was missing. This emptiness was taking me to places of lack of self-worth, disappointment, anxiety, disconnection to my identity, interpersonal relationship problems, and more. To fill in the emptiness, I slowly brought my passion for music, veena, Sanskrit, and Reiki back into my life. This made me feel like I was feeding my mind something more that was unique to myself. Continuing this journey for many years led me to connect with my coach who guided me to discover my purpose: coaching to inspire, educate, and empower people going through self-sabotage and helping them to rise above it and discover peace and purpose in life. Discovering my purpose in life has brought me deeper fulfillment as I live each day purposefully, serving humanity by helping people rise above their emotional pain to discover their authentic self and lead a purposeful life.

Everyone in this world is born unique with unique talents for a reason. This reason is the purpose that shows you the direction in your life. When we have no reason, we lose direction in our life and feel depressed and disappointed. The unique talents that we are gifted with have the power to transform our life but sometimes get hidden under the thick layers of environment, limited beliefs, upbringing, and mental conditioning. Like a miner takes enormous effort and energy to find a diamond under the earth's crust, we must work on ourselves to find the light of purpose that can take us to the destination of peace and happiness.

In Sanskrit this purpose is called dharma. It originates from the word "Dhri"' which means "to hold, bear, or support." One of the meanings of dharma is "sacred duty." It is this dharma that Lord Krishna mentions to Arjuna, the prince and warrior whose duty is to fight for justice and protect the kingdom. Dharma represents the purpose in our life aligned to our Gunas. When your life is based on your dharma, it propels you towards liberation by burning out your desires through egoless action.

According to the ancient Sanatana Dharma, the goals of life are categorized as:

Dharma—living based on your purpose

Artha—wealth for life sustenance

Kama—passion-filled actions

Moksha— freedom from ignorance; authenticity

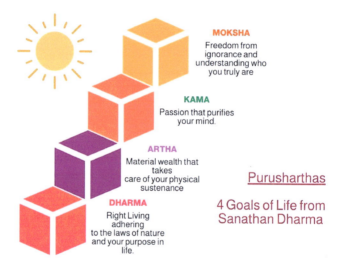

MOKSHA
Freedom from ignorance and understanding who you truly are

KAMA
Passion that purifies your mind.

ARTHA
Material wealth that takes care of your physical sustenance

DHARMA
Right Living adhering to the laws of nature and your purpose in life.

Purusharthas

4 Goals of Life from Sanathan Dharma

When we have discovered our highest purpose in life, which could be our duty, that is aligned to our own personal values or strengths, then we are living our dharma.

Artha represents the internal wealth that is acquired by following your dharma. This wealth does not mean materialistic wealth but the wealth of our personality by utilizing our internal resources. Kama denotes passion that cleanses our mind through egoless actions. Once we live such a life based on Dharma, Artha, and Kama we move into the stage of inner freedom, having identified as our higher selves.

A life of purpose is a life that is meaningful.

When we have a purpose in life, we are able to channel our energy towards a higher purpose that will enable us to elevate our energy and lead a life of satisfaction. There is a shloka from the Holy Bhagavad Gita that says:

श्रेयान्स्वधर्मो विगुणः परधर्मात्स्वनुष्ठितात् ।
स्वधर्मे निधनं श्रेयः परधर्मो भयावहः ।।३५।।

Shreyan swadharmo vigunaha para dharma sva anushti-thath
Svadharme nidhanam shreyaha para dharmo bhaya vahaha

"It is far better to perform one's duty than to perform another's prescribed duty. In fact, it is better to die performing one's duty than to follow the duty of another, which would lead to danger."

Abraham Maslow states that "your life's work is to find your life's work." Are you living your own dharma or following someone else's path?[22]

MEDITATION

Now let's do a short meditation.

- Close your eyes. Sit straight, keeping your shoulders erect. Take a deep breath, and try to focus your attention on the center of your heart as we carry out this guided meditation together.

---

22   The Holy Bhagavad Gita 3:35

- A long-lost friend has sent you an invitation to a meeting. As you have been missing this special friend for a long time, you decide to go and meet your friend. You travel through the roads and the air to meet this special friend. As soon as you reach your friend's abode, you see your friend welcoming you at the doorstep with a sweet smile.
- Tears flow from your eyes, and you hug your friend, as you have missed them. Your friend holds your hand and takes you into a beautiful house. As you enter the house, you see a tall ladder. You climb the ladder slowly, curious to discover what is beyond. The ladder finally takes you to a magical land. As soon as you enter the magical land, you experience that you are in the right place and have been longing to be here. You have all the freedom in the world, and you forget about time. You are at the height of your enthusiasm. You feel like staying here forever. You now see all around things you love and enjoy but had forgotten doing, so you pick them up and bring them down the ladder.
- Now you thank your wonderful friend for showing you the innate gifts within you that you had already possessed but were unaware of possessing. You then promise your friend that you will use your unique gifts to serve humanity and make the world a better place.
-

Based on these Purusharthas, human life can be classified into 4 progressive stages of development or Ashramas:

- Brahmacharya
- Grihastha
- Vanaprastha
- Sanyasa

The ancient Rishis formed this structure to help humankind develop an order for their life that would allow them to evolve through self-development and to eventually reach self-actualization.

- **Brahmacharya:** The stage of Brahmacharya refers to the learning phase where a student takes time to learn from the scriptures and understand the essence they need to implement into their life. With the knowledge gained from Brahmacharya, the student is then ready to move towards the next stage in life.
- **Grihastha:** This stage refers to leading a householder's life, abiding by the duties of taking care of the family and leading a life of harmony. You go to the Vanaprastha stage once the duties are delivered to the family and responsibilities have been completed.
- **Vanaprastha:** In this stage, it is recommended that one practice detachment and self-control to prepare for the stage of Sannyasa, which is to realize oneself.
- **Sanyasa:** In the Sannyasa stage, one becomes prepared mentally and physically to lead a life that serves humanity with a higher purpose for fulfillment. Sanyasa does not just mean wearing a different kind of clothing. Sanyasa is the state of mind of a person who has reached their highest maturity with compassion, love, and acceptance towards all human beings and other living things. You don't have to be part of a particular faith or belief to lead a Sanyasi's life.

PEACE

As mentioned in the Introduction, inner peace was something that I longed for since my childhood. I believed that peace was not something that is achievable for normal people and was meant only for saints. It was when I understood that nothing outside me could be changed that I began looking for alternatives to my emotional pain. Searching for the alternatives moved me in the direction of pursuing my passions and learning various spiritual tools from great teachers, mentors, and coaches. It was only when I began to change the way I perceive, think, feel, and behave that everything around me slowly began to change.

Through introspection, reflection, and guidance from various coaches, I discovered blind spots within my mind that brought me emotional suffering. Later, as I learned and implemented self-management skills from ancient wisdom, I realized that 95% of the problems were created by my own mind. This made me understand that I was the person who was creating my own suffering, and my response to pain determined my suffering. This led me to start cultivating positive responses in my mind and bringing harmony between what I think, say, and do regardless of the person or situation. Numerous times I failed, but every time I failed, I learned new lessons to use for the next time. This eventually became a mental habit to cultivate and restore peace in challenging situations and with difficult people. There are days even today when I slip, but the inner resilience that I have built has shielded me and returns me back to a state of inner peace and balance.

The 4 pillars mentioned above that include mindfulness, mindset, mental discipline, and purpose have not only enabled me to discover peace and resilience but have also transformed the lives of my clients through my 12–week coaching program "Unshakeable Women."

In the coming chapters I will share with you the stories of these unshakable women who have risen from emotional pain and transformed their lives.

REFLECTION

1. What are the activities that you enjoy doing in your day?
2. On a scale of 0–10, what would you rate your enjoyment of each activity? (0 - don't enjoy, 10 - enjoy the most)
3. What enjoyable activities have you given up that you would like to continue if you had the chance to do so today?
4. How will doing these activities make you feel?

CHAPTER 4

PAIN FROM STRESS

"We cannot solve our problems with the same thinking we used when we created them."

- Albert Einstein

Do you experience stress in your life?

In our busy day-to-day life one of the most common occurrences that we encounter is stress. Stress is your body's reaction when you don't have the ability to deal with a challenge. It is a natural feeling and can impact you positively or negatively based on the situation.

Positive stress can help us to move out of our comfort zone and encourage us to take risks to achieve our goals. Going through positive stress can help you feel energetic, motivated, and accomplished. For example, preparing for a concert or exam is a positive stress that would enable you to work harder to perform at your best.

Negative stress can impact your mental and physical health. Negative stress can be induced from the external world triggering our beliefs, thoughts, and emotions, eventually affecting the state of our minds. When we experience negative stress in our life, we usually feel exhausted, frustrated, angry, insecure, lonely, and disappointed.

We all encounter various kinds of stress from acute to chronic stress in our day-to-day lives.

Acute stress stays for a short term and often happens in response to dealing with dangerous situations. Chronic stress can be long term and can include issues around finance or marriage and is considered more harmful as it can result in various diseases.

We all respond to stressful situations in our lives differently. The positive and negative stress that you experience can arise from external sources around you and influence your mind internally. Listed below are some of the common sources of internal and external stressors that are commonly experienced in our lives.

INTERNAL STRESS	EXTERNAL STRESS
UNCERTAINTY	ENVIRONMENTAL ISSUES
WORRY	DEATH OR SEPARATION
FEAR OF FAILURE	CAREER ISSUES
SELF-DOUBT	FINANCIAL ISSUES
OVERTHINKING	PARENTING ISSUES
COMPARISON	RELATIONSHIP ISSUES
PERFECTIONISM	BUSY SCHEDULE

As external stressors cannot be controlled, the only way to manage stress is by focusing on managing the internal stressors that can be controlled so we can continue to lead a stress free and peaceful life. When your internal stressors become unmanageable it leads to anxiety, overthinking, depression, and physical health issues like heart attack, stroke, gastrointestinal problems, chronic back pain, cancer, and more. Taking shortcuts to deal with stress in the form of drugs or smoking or alcohol or people will provide temporary relief but will not help you manage it effectively. So instead of relying on external objects, the most effective way to manage stress is to increase your capability to face challenges by acquiring stress management skills or reaching out to experts such as coaches or therapists who can guide and offer you resources to reduce the impact of stress in your life.

Before I fell chronically ill due to cervical spondylosis, I was going through severe emotional stress from work and relationships in my life. It took more than 10 years for me to change my stressful lifestyle and take steps towards leading a balanced life. Every time I went through severe emotional stress, I noticed my body in pain and suffering. When I observed this pattern happening again and again, I thought I should do something. The first available rescue was my passion for singing. So I chose and pursued it, which brought a huge relief to my stress. Later, I stopped being too hard on myself and began prioritizing myself over everything and everyone around me. This attitude brought a huge difference in my life. The biggest transformation that brought me deeper insights on stress was after reading and understanding the deeper meaning of the message conveyed in Karma Yoga of the Holy Bhagavad Gita. It changed my perspective towards time and work. I began applying the principles and performing work with love and detachment to people and the results. This attitude reduced my stress and also brought me internal freedom. Work became fun that energized me throughout the day and skyrocketed my performance and productivity.

Here are some of the changes that I brought into my schedule that drastically reduced my stress levels with work and family.

Self-care time—Allocate some time during your day for self-care activities. This can include activities that you enjoy doing every day for your mind and body. For example, take some time to read, sing, dance or do whatever makes your heart happy and peaceful.

Connection time—We often become busy during our day and forget the importance of connections. Connections are essential for our mental and physical development. Finding good connections within your family and outside your family will help you manage stress.

Reset time—Dedicate some time during your day for no activity. This means just spending time for introspection without judgment and utilizing this time as a way to unwind from busyness.

Nature time—Nature, as many of us know, is the best healer in the world. Spending time in nature can help us unwind, relax, and ground ourselves.

Playtime—Fun and playtime have become very hard for many of us as they are not regular activities that most of us include in our daily life. However, including fun and play are essential for us not only to learn but also to understand that life is short and not everything needs to be taken seriously. For example - Take some time to play a sport or a game.

Incorporating all of these 5 simple activities within our routine for ourselves, along with time for our mental and physical health, can help us go a long way in this beautiful journey of life. As we have little control on changing the circumstances that cause stress, the only option left to us is to manage stress effectively so that we can lead a life of peace and happiness. When we are better equipped with tools and strategies to manage stress, we can develop mental resilience that will help us cope with various challenging situations in our life and improve our well-being.

REFLECTIONS

1. What are the internal stressors in your life?
2. What are the external stressors in your life?
3. What stress can you remove from your life?
4. What activities can you add to your schedule to help you manage your stress in your daily life?

CHAPTER 5

PAIN FROM UNCERTAINTY

"Uncertainty is the only certainty there is, and knowing how to live with insecurity is the only security."

- John Allen Paulos

HAVE YOU EVER FELT INSECURE with your environment, job, or in your relationships?

As human beings we all prefer to feel safe and secure.

When our safety and comfort is challenged through external threats that arrive through people or events we begin to feel insecure about our lives. We all live in a world of uncertainty and have gone through uncertain situations in our life.

Uncertainty usually happens when external events or things that we can't control occur. When there is certainty, we all know how to prepare for the situation, but when uncertainty creeps in, we are not clear on how the situation may turn out for us. This creeps in as anxiety and worry about our future.

Do you remember the uncertainty that we all ran into with the sudden hit of COVID-19 in 2019?

When the pandemic hit, there was uncertainty about deaths. Uncertainty with travel, vaccinations, various variants, impact of the virus on our health. The uncertainty even raised mental and physical health issues.

Although the uncertainty about when the world would return to fully normal is still not clear, we have still been surviving through it by taking possible preventive measures to protect us. When uncertain situations arise in our lives, some of us develop insecurity about ourselves, relationships, jobs, children, business, and more. When we are in this mode, we are not able to think clearly and make appropriate decisions due to confusion, fear, and anxiety about what might happen in the future.

BEFORE COACHING

Janet was experiencing uncertainty living with her older mother who was diagnosed with cancer. Janet was taking care of her mother all by herself and did not have any support from her family members. Janet had to do the household chores, welcome guests who visited to inquire about her mother, and give medication and attention to her sick mother. As months went by, all these chores began draining Janet mentally and physically. The uncertainty of her future and her mother's health brought in fear and anxiety and made her sleepless at night. Janet reached out to me for help, and we began looking at her situation more closely in order to find better ways to handle it. Janet looked helpless and hopeless. She had a flat and long face that was almost ready to give up. She broke into tears and said, "I don't know what to do," and "This uncertainty is killing me from within." I consoled her and asked her not to worry.

AFTER COACHING

As we went through the coaching sessions on integrating mindfulness, Janet discovered that the options that were available to her were to focus on her present, accept her situation, and do her best rather than worry about the future. She realized that by doing so, she would feel content that she took good care of her mother. When she realized this, I asked her what she should do next, and Janet replied that she should prepare her mindset for the future by looking at the possible alternatives and plan her life accordingly. After having discovered the ways to deal with her uncertainty, Janet felt relieved and began putting this mindset into action. After a few weeks, she told me that focusing on the present took a load from her head, gave her better sleep, and helped her cherish the moments with her mother more deeply.

Some of the ways to handle uncertainty when you do not have clarity about the future are:

1. **Acceptance**—Accept the uncertainty instead of resisting or running away from it. Go with the flow, choosing the best possible approach that works for the present moment.

2. **Pause**—Before you get into autopilot thinking mode, pause and breathe before judging the situation or the person. Ask yourself, "How can I best go through this situation with peace?"

3. **Let go**—Let go of things not in your control. There are people, things, and events that cannot be controlled or changed. Spending time and energy on them will sometimes be futile.

4. **Focus on what you can control**—Focus on the present moment, and do whatever you can to make it the best experience for you. This means focusing on your mindset, actions, skills, and choices that work best for you.

5. **Prepare**—Prepare yourself for the worst-case scenarios with essential resources, skills, and a backup plan required to equip you to face uncertainty at your best.

6. **Surrender**—Believe that everything happens for your highest good, and surrender to the highest will or highest power that operates the world.

None of us have control over our future. What we have control over is only our present moment. Becoming anxious or worried will not improve the situation nor will it allow us to be happy in the present moment. Even if we know this, why then do we still get into a cycle of anxiety, fear, and worry arising from uncertainty?

The reason we do this is because we are too impatient to wait until time reveals it for us. We might think that waiting could bring in an unacceptable change that would disappoint us.

The only way to accept uncertainty is to accept our present moment and go with the flow.

REFLECTION

1. In which areas of your life do you experience the most uncertainty?
   a. Career
   b. Relationships
   c. Health
   d. Other
2. What do you feel is uncertain in the above chosen area?
3. How does the uncertainty affect you?
4. What can you do to reduce the impact of uncertainty affecting you?

CHAPTER 6

PAIN FROM SHAME

"Whatever is begun in anger ends in shame."
- Benjamin Franklin

Do you know shame can affect your emotional health?

Toxic shame is associated with your identity and the feeling that you are worthless. It happens when someone mistreats you, which eventually turns into a belief about yourself. Later, whenever we experience similar situations in life, we begin to react based on these existing beliefs. This feeling arises from our past experiences of being negatively ridiculed, judged, or criticized. Ignoring or neglecting these feelings impacts our relationships and work and damages our identity and mental and physical health. Some ways it can show up in life include anger, fear, withdrawal, and hiding ourselves to protect yourself from danger. Shame freezes us from thinking clearly due to the deep hurt it triggers within us. When we connect the shame to something wrong with us, we begin to suffer and experience emotional pain caused because of it.

However, we can respond to shameful experiences from a place of emotional intelligence. In that case, we can use shameful experiences as an opportunity to stand up for ourselves, guard ourselves against not being affected by it, and be better equipped for next time. Our painful shame experiences are recorded every time they happen, and the scar is not healed unless we take action so that we don't get wounded again.

Whenever I encountered shameful experiences, I blamed myself and became a victim. To prevent them from happening, I used to please the other person by shaming myself without realizing that it would not improve my emotional well-being. One such incident happened a few years back in my workplace where my coworker, who wanted to show his authority and control, began shaming me through humiliating words that almost took me to the point of quitting my job. I consulted my coach to understand if I should consider leaving my job.

Through the coaching sessions, I realized that I should take a different approach to dealing with this coworker rather than run away from facing the situation again. So I stayed at my job and learned different approaches to dealing with this person by understanding his personality. When I understood better that this person was acting from a place of ego and wanted their importance to stand out, I recognized that their actions came from a place of competition and fear. Next time, when the coworker confronted me, I prepared myself and changed my communication style from a place of kindness to a place of a leader ready to fight for themselves and their people. I raised my voice and spoke without fear and with authority to this person, which shut them off. Surprisingly, standing up once made me feel so good that I thought I should continue to do this every time. Eventually, the humiliation from the other person stopped, and I could put off the fire without having to run away from my job, as well as inspire my team members to do the same when they were targeted.

Shaming is one strategy used to make the other person feel down and to reduce their self-esteem so that they will lose belief in themselves and run away due to the fear of being shamed again. It is essential to understand that empathy, kindness, and compassion should be incorporated into our life but not at the risk of hurting ourselves.

There is a story of a saint meditating on the banks of the holy river Ganga. While he was sitting with closed eyes, a scorpion climbed over him and bit him. Someone who noticed it asked the saint, "Why didn't you kill it?" The saint responded that it was the scorpion's nature to bite, and it was the saint's nature to stay calm and react in his way.

In the same way, we don't have to hate or kill the other person who created a shameful experience for us. Instead, we need to approach them differently for our safety.

Spirituality does not mean bearing whatever happens to us; it means rising above the pain and using spirituality's power to guide your path forward. When we communicate or behave from a place of pain, we are in a helpless state that requires attention to ourselves emotionally. It is difficult for us to share and act from a place of strength at that time. You will notice that once you can escape the vicious circle of shame and stand in your own power you can live in your identity without running away from anything that puts your identity at stake.

BEFORE COACHING

Lissy was a married small business owner living with her husband and kids. As Lissy's husband belonged to a different culture, there were compatibility issues with her in-laws. She was considered inferior and not treated respectfully. This caused anger and resentment in her. She was unable to process her feelings and was looking for help. Lissy had tried to maintain physical distance to resolve her issues. However, it did not help her to gain peace and stability of mind.

Before Lissy and I connected on a coaching session, I mentioned to Lissy that all our conversations would be kept confidential. This helped Lissy to slowly open up.

Lissy looked confused and in deep sorrow. She was not sure where to start and how to talk about the emotional battle that she was going through with her husband and her in-laws. I told Lissy to take all the time she needed. After a deep breath and with tearful eyes, Lissy said, "I am feeling stuck, helpless, and lost in my relationship. I have tried everything that I can by pleasing my family and attending to all their needs. In spite of that, my parents and I are not given the respect that we deserve."

Lissy had experienced pain from shame that had impacted her identity and confidence. Her in-laws did not treat her equally, and her opinions were never heard. She was ignored and humiliated before others in the family. This brought Lissy feelings of shame and disappointment. She felt unwanted and not respected in her family, which impacted her relationship with her husband.

AFTER COACHING

I followed a holistic coaching approach to help transformation happen by assisting Lissy in seeing her actual problem underneath the layers of her guilt and resentment. Lissy thought the real problem was her in-laws and her husband. However, by integrating mindfulness–based techniques, Lissy was given profound insight into discovering her true identity. When she realized she couldn't change people around her, and the person who had to change was none other than her, the breakthroughs started happening one after the other. She noticed that there were a lot of self-management skills that she could carry out to maintain her peace and happiness in her family. Some of the most effective practices from ancient wisdom that worked for her were meditation and mindfulness, which helped her to begin the journey to prepare and manage herself for every challenge.

After a few weeks, Lissy came into the session looking relaxed, vocal, and confident. She reflected that after implementing the mindfulness strategies from the previous sessions, she noticed her opinions were more sought after and valued in her workplace and her family.

Lissy continued implementing simple breathing exercises and mindfulness strategies that helped her manage her emotions and develop awareness, self-control, and detachment and that eventually enabled her to establish stable resilience, discover peace, and become confident in her life.

STRATEGIES FOR SHAME

1. **Discover**—Discover your values and true identity.
2. **Establish**—Establish healthy boundaries in your relationships.
3. **Self-Compassion**—Practice self-compassion and be kind towards yourself when you experience shame.
4. **Connect** —Connect with a coach or therapist to develop a positive mindset to overcome shame.

REFLECTION

1. When have you experienced pain from shame?
2. How does shame affect you mentally and physically?
3. What are your internal resources that can help you to overcome the pain from shame? How can you use your values when you experience shame?

CHAPTER 7

PAIN FROM LONELINESS

"If you cannot feel authenticity in your connection, you will start seeing discomfort or loneliness inside. Look for positive energy that allows you to have a positive mindset connection."

- Amritha Kailas

HAVE YOU FELT LONELY IN your life?

According to a global survey conducted by the Statista research department, 33% of the population has been lonely.[23] Many of us know that the pandemic has caused many people to feel lonely. Loneliness is a feeling that is conveyed by our mind. When we do not cater to our mind's needs when it is lonely, it slowly develops into severe mental and physical health issues.

Various research studies show that loneliness is associated with anxiety, depression, suicide, hallucinations, etc. It can also affect the brain's function by affecting neuronal health, cognitive ability, and memory. Loneliness is also associated with poor nutrition, poor habits, and addictions.

We all experience loneliness in many ways. The most common reasons we may feel lonely are when we do not receive love and emotional support from people around us, when we go through

---

23   Statista Research Department, "How Often Do You Feel Lonely?"

grief and loss, and when we become old, sick, or unhealthy. In my personal experience, I have seen the severe impact of loneliness on my grandmother's life, causing her severe depression and eventually cancer. Old age and the emergence of COVID-19 cut her off from social connections. Her desire for belonging was hardly understood, and this developed into mental suffering and other physical ailments later. As social beings, the need to belong is essential for existence, and we all seek it through our relationships in life. When this need is unmet, we begin to feel lonely and get into negative thoughts, habits, and behaviors.

In a world where selfish lifestyles are becoming predominant, we hardly think about making others happy because we always look for others to make us happy. Loneliness cannot be eradicated by placing our happiness on the shoulders of others. The secret weapon is nothing but establishing healthy connections. Healthy connections are essential for our personal development as they help us learn and grow. They also help improve our mental and physical health.

We are all social beings, seeking belonging and love from our relationships around us to lead a happy life. When we do not receive them, we start feeling lonely.

BEFORE COACHING

Lily was a homemaker living in India with her children. She was elderly and sought to belong within her family to feel loved, recognized, and respected. When she did not receive this belonging, she felt she was not wanted and became depressed and unhappy. Although Lily was not financially dependent on her children, she felt her needs were neglected and were not heard. So Lily approached me to help find a solution to her problem.

AFTER COACHING

During the coaching sessions, I taught a mindfulness approach and asked Lily what environment she would want to have in her life instead. She slowly expressed that she wanted to develop a stable mindset where she would not be disturbed when someone responded or behaved in a particular way. As we went through the sessions, Lily mentioned that if she were able to live her purpose in life, it would make her feel happy and content. So we dove into finding Lily's purpose as spiritual mentoring. She shared that doing this made her think that she was acknowledged. Slowly, she discovered she could begin living her purpose with her friends and people who approached her. When she began doing this, she felt less lonely and more content. She created her own circle that included people who wanted her, which took away her attention from overthinking. After dealing with this internal disturbance, her mind was in a much more peaceful state with clarity that allowed her to pursue spiritual opportunities to learn and grow in life.

Here are 4 simple steps to work on your loneliness:

1. **Recognize**—Watch closely the thoughts and emotions that you experience when you feel lonely in your day-to-day life. Please note those thoughts and feelings and the times you experience them the most in your day. For example, it could be on days when you are not at work and have no one to hang out with at home.
2. **Maintain a list of connections**—Maintain a list of connections that can match your values in life. For example, connecting with a friend can make you feel loved, connecting with a coach can make you feel supported, etc.

3. **Map**—Map who can meet your belongingness needs during loneliness and connect with them.
4. **Reflect**—Reflect on your thoughts and emotions after you have spent quality time and energy with someone. Ask yourself: Did this connection help me or not? Is this connection accessible when I need to connect with them?

MEDITATION

Sit straight, and close your eyes.

Take a deep breath.

As you inhale, focus on your breath, and visualize the breath from outside sweeping your entire body from head to toe and touching every cell.

As you exhale, focus on your breath, and visualize your breath filling the entire place around you, your room, your house, your environment, your city, and the world as a whole.

Experience your breath connecting within you and outside you.

You are not alone; you are connected.

As you experience it, say to yourself, "I am grateful for being able to connect within and around me."

Bow down and thank the universe for allowing you to do this meditation today.

Slowly open your eyes.

REFLECTION

1. When do you feel lonely in your life? Please write it down on a scale of 0–10 with 0 meaning "no distress," 5 meaning

"difficult but manageable," and 10 meaning "the most distress I have ever felt."

EVENT	DISTRESS SCALE

2. What actions for each event should you take to help you move down to a lower distress level on the scale? Please write it down on a scale of 0–10 with 0 meaning "no distress," 5 meaning "difficult but manageable," and 10 meaning "the most distress I have ever felt."

EVENT	DISTRESS SCALE

3. How would your life be different if you were able to overcome loneliness?
4. Who do you have around you who can offer you support to overcome loneliness?

CHAPTER 8

PAIN FROM THE PAST

"Your past is just a lesson; don't let it control you."

- Amritha Kailas

A<small>RE YOU STUCK IN YOUR</small> past?

Our past is what determines our present. However, sometimes unpleasant events from our past bother us in the present and take away our peace and happiness. We tend to get into a place of sorrow, guilt, shame, and suffering that eventually eats up our energy and prevents us from progressing into our bright future. Ultimately, this impacts our family, work, friends, and other relationships.

We might not realize that the buried past is causing us problems in our day-to-day life and tend to ignore, avoid, or succumb to activities that will help distract us from it. However, the traumatic effects of the past will continue to show up in our body and mind until we take action to work on them and cleanse them to move forward in our life.

There are 4 simple steps we can take when experiencing past trauma in our lives:

1. **Recognize**—Recognizing our trauma is one of the most challenging steps because it often shows up in our life during unexpected times in the form of body pain, headaches, stomach issues, or feeling upset for no reason. Recognizing

past trauma requires developing awareness when these signals emerge in our body and mind.

2. **Acknowledge**—Acknowledge the signals offered by your body and mind by giving your body and mind the attention it needs at that moment in time. For example, if you are having a headache that was recognized as the residue from your trauma, acknowledge it without judgment.

3. **Initiate**—Ask yourself, "What is the simplest action I can do to help relieve myself from the traumatic experience I am going through now?" For example, it could be initiating simple activities like listening to music that can help you to slowly find calm and relaxation and prevent you from being consumed by the traumatic experience.

4. **Support**—Reach out for support by connecting with a therapist or coach who can help you with tools and strategies that you can implement to overcome the past-related experiences from impacting your present day-to-day activities.

MEDITATION

This is a simple meditation that can help you navigate your focus to the present.

1. **Prepare**—Find a comfortable place at home to relax and ground yourself to work with your past. Take a deep breath in and out at least 3 times until you feel relaxed.

2. **Focus**—Shift your focus internally towards the past inner child who had to endure life's hardships. Pay complete attention to the inner child and stay with it for a few minutes.

3. **Communicate**—Show love and compassion towards the inner child by acknowledging the pain and suffering it had to deal with.

4. **Let it go**—Forgive the inner child for all the mistakes and blunders it has made towards others and you.

5. **Support**—Offer support to your inner child with a statement: "I understand how difficult it is to deal with this pain and suffering, but I'm here to offer you support to outgrow it by providing you with whatever you need from me. We can move past this together."

6. **Visualize**—Imagine a beam of light falling on the inner child and healing it from all the pain and suffering. Take a deep breath, and slowly open your eyes.

We may not be able to fix the events that happened to us in the past. That doesn't mean we have to drain our energy in the present and the future that is still waiting for us to change. Learn from the past, and use it in the present to rebuild a new destiny that awaits you. Life is waiting for you in the present. Allow it to happen. Don't stand in your way, stuck in your past. There is a famous poem in Sanskrit by the great scholar Chanakya that says:

गते शोकः न कर्तव्यः भविष्यं न एव चिन्तयेत् ।
वर्तमानेन कालेन वर्तयन्ति विचक्षणाः ।।

Gathe Shokah na kartvayaha bhavishyam na eva chinthayeth
Varthamanen kaalen varthayanti vichakshanaha

"Don't think about the sorrow of the past nor think and worry about the future. Wise are those who live in the present."

REFLECTION

Imagine your childhood, and write down the positive and negative events that occurred to you which are impacting your present.

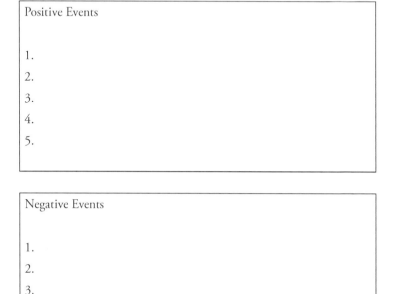

Positive Events

1.
2.
3.
4.
5.

Negative Events

1.
2.
3.
4.
5.

These events have made me become:

Positive Qualities

1.
2.
3.
4.
5.

Negative Qualities

1.
2.
3.
4.
5.

If I overcome my past experiences, I would be able to:

1.
2.
3.
4.
5.

CHAPTER 9

PAIN FROM BETRAYAL

"Nobody can hurt you without your permission."
- Mahatma Gandhi

HAVE YOU GONE THROUGH BETRAYAL in your life?

Betrayal is a harsh feeling, especially when you work your hardest to maintain a good relationship with the betrayer. Very often, we try to retain the tie between us by proving ourselves and pleasing partners in dating or marital relationships. Despite all this, the connection still does not improve, and we feel lost.

The definition of betrayal is the sense of being harmed by a trusted person's intentional actions or omissions. It is caused when someone you trust entirely leaves, hurts, or painfully harms you for their selfish interest. Knowing that you have been betrayed is an excruciating feeling to go through. When we get drowned in this feeling, we become sorrowful and helpless and sometimes start blaming ourselves for being unable to sustain a relationship. This causes self-criticism from trauma-related guilt and shame, which develops into acute mental and physical health issues.

How can you carry on with your life after going through a devastating betrayal?

BEFORE COACHING

Benny was a young woman who went through betrayal from her boyfriend. She felt shameful, angry, and frustrated after the romantic breakup. The pain from the betrayal was so bad that she couldn't focus on her studies, pursue a job, and maintain good relationships with her family and friends. She was confused and directionless.

AFTER COACHING

When Benny came in for the coaching session, she was despondent and in tears as she broke down and shared about the unfortunate incident of betrayal. This young woman came into the coaching session completely lost with little to no hope of moving forward in her life. My words of consolation relieved her, but she was looking for a way out of the feelings of betrayal that were pulling her down and preventing her from achieving her dreams. So I started talking to her from the place of her emotional pain. We began the session with a meditation that included the SIFTE approach described in Chapter 3 where we acknowledged her painful emotions of betrayal, and then she scanned her body to see where the emotions showed up the most. Benny said that she experienced the emotions the most in her chest, and it felt like a hard stab. So we continued working deeper on her emotional pain and exploring ways to clear it.

By the end of the session, Benny had a breakthrough moment and said, "I realize that I need to allow the universe to play its part and allow changes to happen in my life rather than holding onto the past and resisting change."

Once she gained this clarity, she felt relaxed and was ready to move on to work on her dreams that were awaiting her. In the next sessions, Benny and I worked together to find her higher purpose. Towards Benny's last few sessions, she gained deeper insights and wisdom that enabled her to discover her highest purpose, or dharma, of becoming a gymnastics coach. Today, Benny is a successful gymnastics coach, helping women around her and making her family proud.

Here are some steps to move on after going through a betrayal in life:

1. **Accept**—The emotions after betrayal are often painful. They are responses from our brain that inform us that attention is required. Instead of avoiding or ignoring them, take some time to accept them.

2. **Forgive**—After a betrayal, we often start judging our actions and believing we are responsible for everything that has happened. However, instead of criticizing yourself, forgive yourself.

3. **Remove triggers**—The memories from the betrayal are hard to erase and often get triggered in various ways. So it is essential to identify the triggers, and remove them if possible. For example, this includes deleting messages, photos, emails, and social media data that remind you of the incident and lead you to overthink.

4. **Talk it out**—Many times, when we are going through betrayal, it is helpful to consult a coach or a therapist to help feel better and to develop and identify various strategies to overcome the painful emotions and gain clarity on the direction forward.

5. **Celebrate**—Celebrate surviving the betrayal. Take more time for self-care, and use it as an opportunity to give yourself additional love and attention to recover from painful experiences.

6. **Surround**—Surround yourself with support groups, including family and friends, who can courageously help you overcome this situation.

7. **Journal lessons learned**—Look at your experience, and note all the tasks the painful betrayal taught you. For example, make a note of the lessons and the preventive measures that can help protect you from betrayal in the future.

We know our worth more than anybody else. Betrayal or rejection is not an end; it is the beginning of a new journey with an unknown destination waiting for you to conquer. So don't let anyone take your worth away from you. When you live entirely by someone's wishes and not yours, you allow someone else to define you. Instead, take control of your worth to determine how you want to be treated.

MEDITATION

1. Find a suitable time in your day to fall in love with yourself.
2. Close your eyes, and sit straight in a comfortable position.
3. Imagine a bowl in the center of your heart.
4. Visualize love from nature filling the bowl in your heart.
5. Experience the love in your heart, and let it radiate to your mind and body.

REFLECTION

1. What are the lessons that you have learned from your betrayal?
2. What self-care activity can you do to love yourself deeply during the recovery from betrayal?
3. Who are the people who can provide you with emotional support during the betrayal recovery process?
4. What is a new dream that is waiting for you to pursue it as a new beginning?
5. How will you prepare yourself when you begin a new relationship?

CHAPTER 10

PAIN FROM FAILURE

"I have not failed. I've just found ten thousand ways that won't work."

- Thomas Edison

DID YOU KNOW FAILURE IS an essential ingredient for our personal development?

All the great people who have achieved great things in life have failed more times than we can imagine. Thomas Edison failed 10,000 times before inventing the light bulb. However, he did not give up; instead, he continued his learning process until he created the bulb, which became one of the greatest inventions in the world.

Unfortunately, our society talks more about and praises the victories of outstanding accomplishments and less about the lessons of failure that made Albert Einstein, Walt Disney, Mark Zuckerberg, Michael Jordan, Tiger Woods, and many more in this world. If we look at nature, we will notice that even plants and trees adapt during unfavorable rain and winter weather conditions. Everybody in life goes through ups and downs. Most of us become happy when we succeed and sad when we encounter challenges. Some of us even give up on our journey in life, thinking that failure means we are not good enough. We consider the failure of our actions as a failure of ourselves. However, we are not our actions. So labeling ourselves as failures based on our activities is the incorrect interpretation. Every failure comes with a lesson. Failing my driver's exam was one of the most impactful failures that taught me great lessons.

After I moved to Canada, one of the personal goals that I wanted to fulfill was getting a driver's license. I began approaching various driving schools to help me learn, practice, and pass my exams. I looked for the quickest and fastest learning process and chose a driving school to help me get a license in 15 days. The instructor taught me the basic skills, and I took the exam. I failed the exam because I went 5 km/hr above the speed limit in a playground area. I felt humiliated for having committed this silly mistake. The next time I thought I could pass the exam, I decided to learn with a different instructor. So I enrolled in another driving school. The instructor taught me about handling the steering and the controls appropriately this time. So I went for the test again after a few months. This time, I failed again. I missed turning on my left indicator while turning. Again, I felt like something was wrong with me and that I was unfit to get a driving license. This went on 5 times until I came across an advertisement about the AMA driving school, which had the best instructors. I decided to take one more chance before I gave up. I enrolled for AMA driving sessions and had a driving instructor assigned to me.

My driving instructor was patient and understanding. In the first class, he noticed I lacked the specific skills and knowledge required to pass the exam. We developed a deep connection as we discussed spiritual topics during the lesson. He saw that my fear was preventing me from driving successfully. So he told me to work on that and move past it in order to drive calmly. I began working on my mindset, which was fearful and anxious, along with developing my driving skills. My instructor tested me in every class and gave me challenges that were hard but possible to do. For example, when he noticed me being overcautious with speed, he would ask me to increase the speed while staying within the speed limit. This continued, and he made me practice for 6 months by spacing each lesson until I proved eligible to move to the next lesson.

After 6 months, he said, "I am now content with your performance," and he asked me to book my exam. This time, I went for the exam with confidence. I got into the car and listened with full attention to my examiner. I maintained mindfulness as I followed the rules of the road and efficiently carried out all the test requirements without thinking about whether I would pass or fail.

At the end of the exam, I felt very content and inquired about my result. I passed. I was pleased and learnt that failure is essential to progress and succeed. If I had not failed, I would not have been able to identify the weak areas and skills that I had to develop to pass my exam. I felt grateful for having a fantastic driving instructor who changed my perspective towards driving and helped me become a good driver.

There are 7 benefits of failure for our personal growth and development.

1. Provides feedback to help us reflect on our actions
2. Teaches us lessons of perseverance and patience
3. Helps us learn different perspectives on facing a situation
4. Prepares us for adverse situations in our life
5. Builds resilience and grit to undertake challenges
6. Encourages us to work beyond our comfort zone and try new things
7. Helps us develop courage and strength

STRATEGIES TO OVERCOME FAILURE

1. **Acknowledge** your failure.
2. **Disconnect** your failure from yourself—Your failures are not you but the outcome of your actions. Your actions originate from your previous learning, beliefs, and experiences.
3. **Reflect** on your failure—Look at your failure from a distance. For example, if you failed an exam, take some time to reflect on your failure, and note the places where you failed before you took it personally.
4. **Change** the action—If you were given another chance to complete your exam, was there any action that you would do differently? Write down the steps that you would do differently.
5. **Implement**—Use the steps you wrote down, and implement them when you appear for the exam the next time and reflect on your results.

Next time you face failure, welcome it rather than give up. Look at what you can learn from it, and try to grow beyond your limitations again. Failure is not the end; it is just a part of your journey towards your goal. Your mistakes don't define you, so don't let them stop you from reaching your goals.

REFLECTION

1. What is a failure that you recently experienced in your life?
2. What lessons did you learn about yourself and your actions from your failure?
3. What will be your action plan to progress to success?

CHAPTER 11

PAIN FROM GRIEF

"Even grief changes over time."

- Amritha Kailas

HAVE YOU BEEN IN GRIEF?

Grief is a feeling that is associated with the loss of a loved one. Mourning during grief allows us to express our deep emotions for the loved one. This mourning may last for days, for months, or for years. We all know that mourning will not bring the person back to our lives, but the pain of loss can be devastating and unacceptable, especially when it happens unexpectedly. Grief is a place of deep sorrow that arises from our attachment to our loved ones.

I have noticed the severe impact of grief on my grandmother's mental and physical health, which worsened with time. The loss of my grandfather gave rise to her grief in 2015. It slowly led to acute depression and loneliness until she was diagnosed with cancer in 2022. The profound loss was irreplaceable for her. My grandmother was mentally codependent on my grandfather. The loss of my grandfather was not just a physical loss to her but a loss of her identity and purpose, which took away belongingness from her world.

BEFORE COACHING

Dorothy was an educated and intelligent homemaker. She saw vivid dreams of her aunt, whom she had lost in her teens. She was unsure of the reason behind her dreams, but they brought disappointment and fear and affected her close relationships in life. She wanted to leave these negative feelings behind and reached out for my guidance. Dorothy and I began talking deeply about her aunt, and when I asked her about her relationship with her aunt, she broke into deep tears. I allowed Dorothy to take her own time, and when she was ready, she shared that her aunt was a motherly figure. She was the only person in Dorothy's life who loved her unconditionally, gave Dorothy her full attention, and accepted Dorothy as she was without expecting her to change. Her sudden death brought a severe shock to Dorothy's mind. Her parents were concerned about the loss of Dorothy's aunt affecting her health as they occasionally noticed her gasping for breath whenever Dorothy remembered her. So they relocated to a different city to help her forget and move past it. Over the next 15 years after the loss, Dorothy suppressed the grief, which affected her sleep and health. When she had dreams of her aunt, her relatives told her that her life was at risk and that her aunt would take her life. So she began hating her aunt and resisting the dreams. This increased the stress in her mind.

When I heard this, I asked Dorothy, "What would your aunt wish for you now?" Dorothy said that her aunt would want her good. I asked Dorothy, "What could be the reason that your aunt is coming in your dreams?" Dorothy broke down into tears and confided that she didn't have anyone around her who loved her unconditionally. When she saw her aunt in her dreams, she felt like she was being accepted, though she had been told to reject her. She said, "It has been hard for me as I have not been able to grieve her loss and come to terms with it." Dorothy slowly realized that she had to give herself time to accept the grief to move forward.

AFTER COACHING

After a couple of sessions, when I reconnected with Dorothy, she said she was so grateful that she could remove the internal block from her mind after 15 years, allowing her to look into her deeper self with much more clarity. Dorothy also mentioned that the dreams of her aunt no longer bothered her, and she could sleep well and focus on her goals in her life more effectively.

Based on the 3 Gunas we discussed in Chapter 3, grief falls under the category of Tamo Guna and leaves us in a mental state of passivity. This means that our minds will be unable to carry out actions actively and will need time and assistance from people around us to navigate to a place of an active state.

An article published in PsychCentral shares 5 stages of grief based on the Kübler-Ross grief cycle.[24] Only some people go through all 5 steps, and some may remain in one stage longer.

FIVE STAGES OF GRIEF

The 5 stages are denial, anger, bargaining, depression, and acceptance.

Denial includes the stage where the loss of a loved one, through death or separation or sickness, brings the shock of something unexpected that has happened.

Anger comes in after denial causing you to wonder why this situation occurred to you and not others around you.

---

24   Casabianca, "Mourning and the Five Stages of Grief."

Bargaining comes in after anger. It is where you begin to feel guilty and consider if you could have saved the person if you had done things differently.

Depression is when you understand that the person you loved dearly is no longer around you, and you begin to feel deep sadness.

You might show withdrawal from the real world, hopelessness, and suicidal thoughts.

Acceptance is when you are ready to move on after accepting the hard reality of the loss. It is essential to understand that to reach this stability, mental effort is required to be able to come to an agreement with the loss and be able to gain the mental strength to move forward and live in reality. In the great epic *Ramayana*, written by the great sage Valmiki, the grief of Kausalya, the queen and mother of Lord Sri Rama, is depicted when Lord Sri Rama departs from the kingdom to the forest.

Dasaratha, the King of Ayodhya and father of Sri Rama, gives the order to exile Sri Rama to the forest based on his promise to one of his evil wives, Kaikeyi. Dasaratha loves Sri Rama very dearly. However, he becomes helpless before the stubbornness of Kaikeyi and is forced to execute the order. When Kausalya hears that Sri Rama is going to the forest, she goes into a phase of grief and anger, leading to cursing words towards her husband and King Dasaratha.

Later, when she realizes that the exile was not his fault, she realizes her mistake and says:

शोको नाशयते धैर्य, शोको नाशयते श्रृतम् ।
शोको नाशयते सर्व, नास्ति शोकसमो रिपुः ॥

Shoko naashayathe dhairya shoko naashayathe shritham
Shoko naashayathe sarvam naasthi shoka samo ripuhu

"Sorrow kills one's patience; sorrow makes one forget one's ability to distinguish between good and evil; sorrow takes away all good qualities, and thus, sorrow is the biggest enemy of an individual."

Thus, one should not give themselves over to the hands of sorrow. Recovering from grief takes time and effort. We all come into this world for a definite time and purpose. There are some factors we do not have control over in our life, including aging, death, having poor health from diseases, natural calamities, or accidents. These are the times when we realize that our ego or money does not have the power to recreate a life. It is essential to understand that our environment, which includes people we love, can move out of our lives anytime, which is not in our control. We only have control over our interactions with people when they are alive. After they are gone, we only have memories.

So cherish every moment you live with your loved ones because age and health will not return. Be grateful for the love and service your loved ones provide you, and return it the best way possible as you may not get the same chance again when they are gone from your life. In the Holy Bhagavad Gita, when Arjuna shows resistance to fighting against his cousins, Lord Krishna mentions that the soul never perishes, and the body ages and dies. Based on the accumulations of Karma of the soul, it may be reborn through another body in the same world or enter other worlds that are unknown or inaccessible to our minds. If the soul has achieved self-mastery or realized oneness with the higher power, the soul will not be reborn and will become a guiding light to the world.[25]

For this reason, it is essential to lead a life of purity within our minds and do whatever we can for the people around us so

25   Joshi, "Today's Subhashita," Sanskrit Subhashitas.

that the world will remember and thank you even after you are gone. Like a flower that spreads its fragrance and then fades away, may we all be able to give the world what we have as we cannot take anything in our hands when we leave. Grief is unavoidable in all our lives. When a lady approached Gautama Buddha, grieving over the death of her husband, Buddha told the lady to collect mustard seeds from a house where nobody had lost a loved one. She returned empty-handed because there was no one house where they had not lost someone in their lives. This experience made the lady understand that life is short, and everybody goes through grief in different ways in their lives.

Nobody prepares for grief as it is not something we expect or want to happen. However, it is essential to build resilience to face grief realistically. This does not mean becoming hard-hearted; that does not mean you have matured.

The steps that you can take when you encounter grief are:

1. **Acknowledge** that you have gone through loss—It is challenging to accept the loss, especially if it has happened unexpectedly. It might affect us profoundly through our strong emotions and attachment towards our loved ones. So acknowledge that grief is inevitable for everyone and that your loss is not replaceable.
2. **Find support**—Grief takes us to a state of loneliness and depression. So find a suitable coach or therapist who will listen to you and guide you without judgment to help you navigate through grief smoothly.
3. **Return**—Your loved one likely taught or modeled a way of life before you. Although they are gone, continue their activities or service to express gratitude towards your lost loved one.

By following the above activities, grief will not consume you and will help you move forward in your life. Everyone has their journey in this world. When the time comes, we have to go, and there is no return. Why not make this journey a memorable one for yourself and others? Grief needs time and space to heal, but do not let it take away your journey from you, as that is the best way you can show your deep love for your lost loved one.

MEDITATION

1. Sit in a comfortable place, and close your eyes.
2. Focus your attention on the center of your heart and imagine your loved one in front of you.
3. Give space for your grief, and give it your full attention.
4. Notice if there are particular areas in your body where you feel the grief the most.
5. Stay focused on the area where you experience grief the most, and talk to your grief as you would speak to a close friend.
6. Please take a deep breath, and visualize the breath moving to your grief and clearing it slowly.

REFLECTION

1. What is the most recent grief that you have experienced in your life?
2. Who are the people who can offer you support during the grieving period?
3. What activities can help you heal your grief?

CHAPTER 12

PAIN FROM COMPARISON

"Comparison is the thief of joy."
- Theodore Roosevelt

Do you compare yourself with others?

As I was growing up, one of the biggest factors that led to my development of self-doubt was comparison between me and my sibling, me and my peers, me and my cousins, and more. Every time I was compared, I began believing that something was wrong with me and that I needed to be like someone else to be accepted. This led to people pleasing and a craving for validation that I carried for many years, which impacted my self-esteem and eventually led to my unhappiness.

Comparison is a behavior that we learn from the people around us early in our life. Nothing in this world is the same. The creator of the universe made each one of us different so that we can all exhibit uniqueness and contribute to the glory of the world. It is impossible to be the same as another person. We can learn and develop qualities that another person has but cannot be the same as them. There are differences in our intelligence, capabilities, skills, emotions, and qualities within us, all of which contribute to the mindset, behavior, and success of a person. A fish cannot be compared with an elephant. Nothing is less important in this world. A fish contributes in its own way, as does the elephant. However, with the rise of comparison around us, including on social media, we believe whatever we see and think that we are not as good as other people, which may or may not be true. When we do that, we deny the capabilities within us and neglect the possibilities that can arise from us when we focus on our own values and strengths that make us who we are in this world.

Dharme is living a life that is tuned to who you are and your purpose in this world. There is a popular quote in the Holy Bhagavad Gita that says, "Sva Dharme Nidhanam Shreya Paradarmo Bhayavah." This means it is better to do your purpose because doing someone else's purpose would result in danger.

Most comparisons lead to unhealthy thinking habits, which in turn lead to jealousy, anger, and more.

When we experience these feelings, instead of going by the feelings, take a moment to think:

1. Why am I having these feelings? (Ex: I am having these feelings because that person looks happier than me.)
2. What is it that makes me become jealous of them? (Ex: Their calmness and resilience towards different situations in life.)
3. What can make me not feel jealous? (Ex: Becoming happy and peaceful like them.)
4. What should I do about that? (Ex: I should start working towards it.)

Simple self-talk can help us avoid becoming trapped in negative emotions and becoming helpless. If we manage our emotions as soon as they arise within us, we will be able to think clearly and utilize the energy towards developing ourselves by focusing on ourselves rather than someone outside us. We begin to compare ourselves when people around us do or have something different from us. This arises from a place of scarcity in us around the object of comparison. As soon as we notice it and believe it, we begin the process of comparison, sometimes even without any reason.

Everyone has a unique path in life with different intentions, ambitions, knowledge, skills, and capabilities. When we see someone who does not have the same scarcity, we believe they are better than us, which will eventually make us feel lower than them, envious, and angry towards them. The scarcity can be in the form of knowledge, wealth, success, physical looks, emotional states, skills, talents, family, children, properties, social media pictures, and more. Whatever we believe is the source of comparison, it makes us feel uncomfortable from within and results in self-doubt. It is important to understand that someone possessing or doing something that we don't have or do does not in any way mean that we are not as good as them. It only shows the outcome of the hard work or effort that they have put into life, which has been realized in different ways.

One way to look at comparison differently is by looking at it as a source of inspiration for us to learn from others and understand their journey that could have helped them to bridge the gap that they once had in their life. When we use comparison for personal growth, it helps us to move forward. When we use comparison to entertain envy, hatred, and anger, we move downward into self-doubt and become stuck.

BEFORE COACHING

Recently, I had a client, "Marley," who mentioned that she felt really uncomfortable with people who were smarter than her.

She mentioned that this made her feel she was not good enough and made it hard for her to have authentic conversations. She felt very conscious about herself not making mistakes while talking or behaving before these people, and it made it uncomfortable for her to present information in the right way, leading to awkward moments.

AFTER COACHING

While going through the coaching sessions, Marley realized that these feelings arose from within her because she did not know much about the areas that were discussed during those conversations, which made her feel stupid or dumb.

Progressing through the sessions, she recognized that she had similar areas of expertise, and not knowing one area did not mean that she was dumb but instead showed an opportunity for her to learn from the other person. She also realized that saying "I don't know" did not mean she was not good enough. It just meant that she had not known this information until now. One of the powerful ways that she decided to implement this understanding was by understanding who she truly was based on her strengths, acting from that place, and then asking questions to the other person rather than comparing herself negatively and dwelling in self-doubt.

STEPS TO OVERCOME COMPARISON

1. **Self-Acceptance**—Accept yourself and your life situations as they are currently.
2. **Gratitude**—Be grateful for all the small and big blessings you have in your life rather than your shortcomings.

3. **Focus on personal strengths**—Your values and strengths are your unique assets. Focusing on these would help you not to be distracted from comparison.

4. **Positive self-talk** —Develop a practice of talking positively to yourself when you notice yourself getting into a place of comparison.

5. **Find support**—Connect with a coach or a therapist to receive personal guidance, motivation and support regularly to help you move forward without getting stuck in comparison.

The creator of this world instilled divine intelligence in every little being, including us. Our incomparable uniqueness in us is what makes us more special than any other person in this world. Our diversities in us do not mean something is wrong with us. Instead, it means there is something in us that matters the most in this world. When we compare, we are questioning the innate gifts presented to one person from another.

Our quest to enrich our lives and become perfect makes us compare ourselves with others.

We cannot stop others from comparing us, but we can stop comparing ourselves.

Comparison is a denial of our power with reliance on others.

Compare yourself today with who you were yesterday.

REFLECTION

1. Who do you usually compare yourself with?
2. What does the person you compare have different from you?
3. How can you change your comparison into inspiration?

CHAPTER 13

PAIN FROM SELF-DOUBT

*"If you hear a voice within you say you cannot paint, then
by all means, paint and that voice will be silenced."*
- Vincent van Gogh

HAVE YOU EVER FELT THAT you are not enough?

This is one of the beliefs that many of us carry for a long time.
My feelings of believing that I was not enough began when I was
a toddler and remained with me for more than 30 years. There
were numerous challenges that I had to experience to realize that
my self-worth was not dependent on anyone else other than me.
I had valued everyone else but myself for most of my life and
realized that it was because I relied on others for decision-making,
approval, and consent.

One of the greatest gifts bestowed on us is the ability to think
and discriminate. This unique ability differentiates us from other
living beings on this beautiful planet. However, when we lose the
power of discrimination, we are consumed by our inner voices that
steal peace from our lives. These inner voices can suck our energy
and leave us paralyzed. Self-doubt arises from a lack of belief in
oneself and deep fear. Many factors lead to self-doubt, including
past experiences, toxic relationships, and more. Self-doubt, when

not fixed, can lead to severe mental and physical health issues, which include depression, anxiety, overthinking, procrastination, impostor syndrome, and more. When we face various challenges in life, we begin to doubt our ability to protect ourselves in dangerous or threatening situations. Although this may not be the ideal solution, repeating this pattern over time leads us to blame ourselves before we take action.

All that we think is not true. The inner critic or the negative voice that chatters within us often drowns us in misery or sorrow. It is hard to recognize the inner critic as it arises from our experiences and limited beliefs. When left unresolved, it impacts our mental health adversely, causing overthinking, self-doubt, depression and anxiety. These negative voices are unreal and cause noises inside our minds, distracting us from achieving our true potential.

In an article published by *Psychology Today*, it is estimated that nearly 85% of people worldwide suffer from self-doubt.[26]

Self-doubt can impact our identity adversely and cause damage to it because it arises from doubting the capabilities that constitute ourselves. When we experience self-doubt, we put ourselves lower than others in our relationship. This makes us believe in others and rely on their identity. Living such a life for a more extended period of time slowly causes us to lose our identity, which is an understanding of who we are. Self-doubt can also affect our thinking, relationships, and performance at work.

सुखदुःखे समे कृत्वा लाभालाभौ जयाजयौ ।
ततो युद्धाय युज्यस्व नैवं पापमवाप्स्यसि ॥ ३८॥

Sukha Dukhe same kritva laaba labou jaya jayou
Tato yudhaya yujyasva naivam papam ava pyasi

---

26   Guttman, "The Relationship With Yourself."

"Look at happiness and sorrow the same as success and failure. So fight for the purpose of the war, and you will not incur the bad effects of it."

After mentioning this, Lord Krishna states that the only way to overcome suffering is to develop equanimity of mind.

कर्मजं बुद्धियुक्ता हि फलं त्यक्त्वा मनीषिणः ।
जन्मबन्धविनिर्मुक्ताः पदं गच्छन्त्यनामयम् ॥ 51॥

Karmajam budhi yuktha hi phalam tyaktva maneeshinaha
Janma bandha vinirmuktha padam gachantyanamayam

"The wise person with the equanimity of intellect carries their duty without being attached to the results. Therefore, they become free from bondage of life and death and overcome suffering."[27]

Having listened to Lord Krishna's advice to develop detachment, Arjuna, with a mind of curiosity, asks Krishna: "What is the personality of a 'perfect man' who is able to establish equanimity?"

Like Arjuna, we all provide numerous excuses to convince ourselves and others not to execute our duties or responsibilities in various situations. So how can we get over our self-doubt?

BEFORE COACHING

Ginny was an educated, talented homemaker. Ginny lived with her husband. Ginny had dreams to start her own business and live a life of confidence and independence. She had to pass exams that

---

27   The Holy Bhagavad Gita 2: 38, 51

would help her receive certifications that were required to achieve her dreams. However, she was looking for external validations that would confirm that she would pass her exams. So she reached out to a tarot card reader to know if she would pass the exam if she appeared for it. The first tarot card reader said she would pass. However, Ginny was not convinced, so she went to another. This time, the tarot card reader said she would fail. This deepened self-doubt in Ginny. So she went to another tarot card reader, and they also said that she would fail her exams. Ginny became very upset and disappointed. She decided to bring up this topic during the coaching sessions with me. We began our discussion and went deeper into her beliefs that led to self-doubt and made her look for external validation.

AFTER COACHING

Eventually, we arrived at a place where Ginny realized that the person who had control over her destiny was her and not the tarot card reader. So with this new realization, Ginny began working towards her exam with the tools that I had offered her to manage her self-doubt, thinking, and emotions. She appeared for her exam with good preparation, and later, when she came for the session after a few weeks, she shared that she had passed the exam with 95%. Ginny was very happy that she was able to move one step closer to her dream regardless of the tarot card readers' opinion. At the end of the session, she smiled and said, "How did I believe that someone else would know about my future? I am the one who knows about me more than anyone else in this world."

STRATEGIES

1. **Identify negative statements.**
   What are the statements that sabotage you from achieving your goal? For example, make a list of all the statements that put you down in the form of "I am not good enough," "I can't do this," "I will end up being ridiculed," "I will be judged," "I will fail," etc.

2. **Zoom into your triggers.**
   What situation or event triggers the statements that you have identified? Include the triggers in your list that include people, events, and conditions which bring up the self-sabotage statements in your head.

3. **Validate evidence.**
   Use your power of discrimination to validate these thoughts with evidence before believing them. For example, asking questions to yourself to understand the statement's validity could be like: "What are the reasons that prove that 'I am not good enough'? Is it valid?" You can also use your past experiences to assess the truth.

4. **Challenge statements.**
   Challenge the identified statements. For example, consider what is the worst that could happen if you deny the self-sabotage statements and carry out the action?

5. **Perform a simple activity that invalidates the negative statements.** Perform a small part of the action to take you towards your goal. Consider what simple steps you can execute to invalidate your inner noise.

When we place our trust in others more than ourselves, then we give importance to their opinions to determine our reality. It is not bad to listen to other opinions if they are good and help us to move forward. However, they can keep us stuck in places of self-doubt and living a life believing that someone else is responsible for making things happen in our life.

Believe in yourself because if you don't believe no one else will.

REFLECTION

1. What self-doubt statements have stopped you from chasing your dreams?

2. In what areas of your life have you seen yourself projecting self-doubt? (Work, relationships, or other places?)

3. What can you do to rise above your self-doubt and achieve your dreams?

CHAPTER 14

PAIN FROM OVERTHINKING

"What you think of yourself is more important than what other people think about you."

- Seneca

YOUR ASSUMPTIONS DISTORT YOUR REALITY. The more you assume, the more you move away from the truth.

Has overthinking prevented you from achieving your goals and finding peace?

Overthinking is overburdening ourselves with thoughts that arise from our imagination that are beyond our control in the present. The accuracy of the predictions we make from them may not be helpful for us in our current situation in life. In this state of mind, we tend to get stuck in our thinking based on solid beliefs and conditioning. This prevents us from taking healthy risks and eventually leads us to a place of disappointment. Overthinking arises from fear of threat or danger that can affect us. Chronic overthinking develops into mental health issues that include anxiety and depression. According to *Forbes*, 73% of people between the ages of 25–35 are affected by chronic overthinking, along with 52% of the people between the ages of 45–55.[28]

BEFORE COACHING

Emily was a small business owner living with her husband and child in Canada. Emily struggled to have authentic conversations with her spouse, friends, and potential clients because she felt she was not lovable and worthy enough. So whenever she was conversing with them, her mind used to take her to a place where it would chatter, "They won't like you" or "They are going to think you are stupid." These thoughts prevented her from making good friends and having a good relationship with her family. When Emily and I connected through the coaching sessions, I dove deeper into her feelings of being unlovable. We discovered that as a child, Emily's parents never provided her love and support when she most needed it, and she was always hurt when she demanded love. So later on, when she interacted in her relationships, the same old thoughts were triggered.

---

28 Santilli, "How to Stop Overthinking."

AFTER COACHING

I asked Emily, "If your mind was a person, would you hang out with them?" Emily immediately replied yes because she recognized that she had all the positive qualities required for someone to love her. Towards the end of the session, Emily realized that her mind was trying to protect her in social situations because of her past experiences where she was hurt when she attempted to connect and have meaningful relationships. So Emily said that when these thoughts came "I can do something about it. I know I am lovable, and there are qualities in me that make me adorable. My mind is trying to protect me because I have been hurt before, but that's not true now. So I can recognize that thought as a passenger. 'Unlovable' is coming to protect me, but I don't need them, and they are invalid. If it is not true, I won't believe it or engage in that thought, and I will give an example instead to make my mind understand and move on."

So how can we stop overthinking?

Here are 4 simple strategies to stop overthinking:

Accept—Develop an attitude to question the thoughts that arise in your mind based on facts before believing them completely, and entertain only the thoughts that confirm the validity based on your analysis.

Retrain—Not all thoughts are urgent or important enough to pay attention to in the present moment. So if a thought comes about the future or past, retrain your mind through self-talk to postpone it for a later time.

Engage—Often, we overthink when we are idle or less occupied in our daily life. Notice when you often get into the overthinking mode, and find a way to engage in any activity that shifts your thinking into an immediate action that needs focus and attention.

Recharge—Take moments in your day to free yourself by relaxing your mind and body. For example, incorporate activities that include meditation, music, exercise, and nature walks to relax your mind and body.

By performing the 4 strategies above, we are training our minds to move from overthinking to a state of action that will eventually lead to success and happiness. So the next time you begin overthinking, redirect your creative energy instead of allowing yourself to go into depletion. In the Holy Bhagavad Gita, when Arjuna is unable to control his mind, Lord Krishna says:

असंशयं महाबाहो मनो दुर्निग्रहं चलम् ।
अभ्यासेन तु कौन्तेय वैराग्येण च गृह्यते ।। 35।।

Asamshayam mahabaho mano durnigraham chalam
Abhyasena tu kaunteya vairagyena cha grihyathe

"It is definitely difficult to control your mind, but with practice and detachment, you can definitely gain control over it."[29]

> **"Overthinking will not solve your problem, it will only paralyze you." - Amritha Kailas**

REFLECTION

1. In what situations do you find yourself overthinking?
2. How has overthinking affected your life?
3. What steps can you take towards retraining your mind during overthinking?

---

29   The Holy Bhagavad Gita 6:35

CHAPTER 15

PAIN FROM PEOPLE PLEASING

"If you know your worth, you don't have to prove your worth."

- Amritha Kailas

HAVE YOU EVER FELT TIRED of pleasing people in your life?

People pleasing means expressing kindness or favor towards someone and living up to their expectations so that they like you. It is a form of external validation in which we look up to people around us so that they accept, recognize, and like us so that we feel a sense of belonging. Many of us have fallen into this trap from childhood, believing that if we live up to the expectations of our loved ones, we will be able to lead a happy and peaceful life. However, we tend to forget that in this process, we fail to live a life for ourselves. We are allowing others to determine how we think, act, and behave. This slowly leads us to a place where we ignore our inner voice or intuition and enable others to take charge of our life. Prolonged people pleasing can cause dissatisfaction, resentment, and depression, leading to unhappiness.

People pleasing arises from a lack of self-esteem, fear of rejection. and sometimes also from past trauma. As something we learn over time becomes part of our beliefs, there are ways to overcome traumas to lead a life of authenticity.

Six simple strategies can help us overcome external validation.

1. **Identify**—Find out the 4 W's—when, where, what, and who—of where you have been seeking external validation from your life. For example, I often used to seek external validation from my loved ones while making an important decision because I used to consider others experts based on their age and seniority. Whenever I was denied approval, I used to feel lost and helpless. So identifying these people and situations from your past can help you understand the control you have provided them as you sought approval.

2. **Prepare**—Prepare yourself to accept rejections from your loved ones that you once looked up to before performing actions. Accept that rejection is part of being different and unique.

3. **Establish boundaries**—Create healthy boundaries for yourself before jumping into performing actions for approval. For example, this could be as simple as asking: Do I have the resources and time to perform this action? Do I have to sacrifice my own needs to do this action? Or will taking this action serve me in the future or make me feel sad?

4. **Prioritize**—Prioritize your voice over others regarding critical events and decision-making. This does not mean not listening to other opinions, but it does mean listening in an unbiased way where you can consider the input as data or facts required for making your own decision.

5. **Learn to say no**—Sometimes saying no seems complicated. However, it is a powerful word that helps you to give yourself

enough time, space, and freedom to respect your choices, eventually allowing you to develop strong self-esteem.

6. **Take risk**—Assess the risk of acting based on your inner critic. For example, you can ask questions like, "What is the worst thing that can happen if I follow my inner voice and take action?"

Being you is the most unique and wonderful gift in the world. When we begin to listen and act based on our values and intuition, we can live an authentic life where freedom of thought and expression are no longer a dream but a reality.

Live your best life as your best self!

REFLECTION

1. Who have you found pleasing most of the time?
2. What do you expect from others while pleasing people?
3. What can you do next time when you find yourself pleasing people?

CHAPTER 16

PAIN FROM RELATIONSHIPS

"Hold onto your reins as you sail through your relationship."
- Amritha Kailas

CODEPENDENCY

When we get into a relationship, we carry our identity along with us, and based on our experiences, we may or may not be able to live in that relationship based on our identity.

It is when we cannot live our identity in a toxic environment that we begin to feel helpless, unwanted, sad, and discouraged. However, we sometimes forsake our identity to maintain the peace of the family, which means giving up ourselves.

Every human being is born to achieve their true purpose in life. Relationship ties were created to satisfy our need to belong in this community. This does not mean that one has to give up their identity to fulfill the requirement of belongingness. When we lead a life where we no longer know who we are after being in a relationship, we end up disappointed. Pleasing or satisfying others will not help us to regain our identity. Only when we regain control of our life and discover who we are can we live a life in our true identity. While growing up, I had the privilege to be surrounded by my grandparents, who were one of the pillars of strength in my life. My grandmother was a kind and loving woman who served unconditionally. Although she was educated and employed, she was codependent on my grandfather. Everything for her was fine until my grandfather passed away. She could not stand his absence and considered that there was no purpose left before her as a hope to live in this world. She believed her identity depended on him; his passing away had taken it from her. However, in reality, our mental attachment makes us think that our identity is based on others.

You are unique and capable of achieving incredible things in life. Don't burn your identity to save a relationship or your family's peace because once you have lost your identity, you have lost everything in you. We encounter an identity crisis when we enter a new relationship, a new career, or go through a loss. This happens when our identity is challenged.

BEFORE COACHING

Nancy was going through severe emotional pain due to rejection from her husband, which included him ignoring her and treating her without respect. She had tried pleasing her husband by carrying out all the household chores, offering gifts, and through financial support. Regardless, she was not recognized and was blamed for her faults from her past. In order to establish peace in her family, Nancy began burying her identity and her needs. Compromising her identity to sustain her relationship drained her energy and led her towards overthinking and disappointment.

When Nancy came for the coaching sessions with me, she was extremely fed up and wanted to just quit her marriage as all the pleasing that she did was draining her energy and peace of mind.

She was deeply concerned that living in such a state would lead her to mental and physical health issues. She felt helpless, frustrated, and stuck.

AFTER COACHING

As we began the sessions, we explored deeply into her relationship and discovered that the emotional pain that she was suffering from arose from not receiving the love, care, and emotional support that she longed for in her relationship. She noticed that the only value that she received from her relationship was security and social status. She began crying when the harsh reality stood before her. When Nancy was ready to continue with the session, I asked her, "Who is able to give you the love and care that you are looking for?" She smiled and said, "Me. I need to love myself and take care of myself." She wiped her tears and said, "Yes, I have made mistakes, but my partner has, too. I have forgiven him, but he is not able to forgive me. It is not my fault. I need to focus on myself and find my happiness rather than chasing him to make me happy." She charted out her new routine with personal time for self-connection and self-care. In the later coaching sessions, Nancy learned mindfulness strategies to integrate into her relationship. Eventually, Nancy realized her true identity, learned to set healthy boundaries, changed her communication style, and began living by her personal values in life. With this newly derived internal strength, Nancy continued in her relationship as a new, empowered woman.

One of the most common mistakes that we all make, especially women, is to tolerate and take all the blame on ourselves for maintaining relationships even when we see the other person's mistakes. When we take the blame, we are spoiling our mental strength and not helping the relationship grow. It is essential to step into your identity and be who you are, even in your relationship, because you will not find happiness otherwise.

Three simple ways exist to retain your identity and maintain a healthy relationship. The 3 ways are:

1. **Establish boundaries**—Healthy boundaries allow you to create space for yourself to think independently about areas of your life that can seriously impact your identity when not taken care of. These areas can include self-care, health and wellness, personal growth, and development. For example, one of the boundaries that has been respected and agreed upon by my husband and me is the nonconsumption of meat. This has allowed me to live by my principles while giving freedom to my husband to live according to his food choices.

2. **Create personal time**—Dedicate some time during your day to spend alone with yourself and carry out a hobby that allows you to pursue your passions, which are your unique gifts in life, and tap into your incredible potential. For example, my husband and I have different hobbies and pursue them differently. Dedicating personal time to ourselves has helped us grow in our areas of interest without interfering with each other.

3. **Live by your values**—Values are external representations of our character and influence our actions. When we are aware of our values in life and live accordingly every day, we develop stronger personalities that can bring new perceptions into our life. For example, the 3 central core values I try to live by daily in my family and at work include kindness, patience, and perseverance. Living by these values has always helped me stay grounded and choose activities that align with my daily values.

By following these 3 simple daily strategies, you will notice that you can maintain your identity while being in your relationship and catering to your family's needs. A beautiful relationship needs differences to grow and flourish as it gives an opportunity to allow us and our partners to have open communication, maintain a unique identity, and positively support each other in running a family together.

Through this collaboration, you are building a strong family and setting a realistic example to your children, enabling them to make a stronger family in the future.

In life, opportunities brought to us by time cannot be recreated. So let's rebuild love and peace into our families before it is too late.

"When you stop expecting people to be perfect, you can like them for who they are." - Donald Miller

COMMUNICATION ISSUES

Most of us obey traffic rules when we are on the road to prevent accidents with other vehicles. However, how often do we follow rules of communication to avoid verbal accidents in our workplaces or homes?

Each of us in this world is unique and has a unique path in life. We are all traveling to different destinations. What will happen when we don't pay attention to our own thoughts, which are the signals from the outside world? We end up in a collision. We all go through good and bad thoughts in our everyday life. It's only when we become aware of our thoughts as we would at a traffic signal that we will be able to act consciously without causing harm to us or others around us.

Words are tools that are provided to us in the world to communicate with other fellow beings. Words originate from our thoughts and carry emotions. Thoughts carry energy, and this energy is transferred into our emotions and words. When we think negatively, we create negative energy. However, we pay very little attention to the words that we use in our conversations especially at home or in the workplace. Why do we have to pay attention to our own words?

Each word that we put out into the world is an expression of our own self. Sometimes we unconsciously throw out negative words to another person, thinking it will hurt them. However, according to Newton's third law, every action has an equal and opposite reaction. So every negative thought that is transmitted out to someone actually harms us and not the other person. Let's take an example of us getting angry and shouting at someone, using rude words. Based on the emotional intelligence of the other person listening to us, they may or may not feel upset. However, the rude words that originated from us have the negative emotion of anger attached, which produces toxic chemicals in our body and then transmits toxicity to every organ in our body, thereby creating negativity within us. This eventually leads to severe physical illness and can result in chronic diseases.

Having understood this connection, what can we do?

I am going to share with you a simple technique that will help you respond rather than react to situations. There are 3 stages to this technique.

The 1st stage is called **Preparation.**

1. **Preparation**—This stage involves preparing your mindset during the communication process. The steps in the preparation process are:

a. **Stop**—In this step, take a moment to stop judgment and reaction. You can use any kind of reminder that will help you to stop before you say anything.

b. **Pause**—Pause for a moment by imagining you are stepping back one step, and use breathing or a counting exercise.

The 2nd stage is called **Planning.**

2. **Planning**—In this stage, imagine you are wearing your thinking hat and ask the following questions of yourself:

a. Who am I talking to?

b. What is the final outcome that I am looking for from this conversation?

c. Where am I talking?

d. Is this the best time for me to talk?

e. Why do I think I need to talk? Will it help the final outcome?

The 3rd stage is **Execution.**

3. **Execution**—In the execution stage, use the answers from **Planning** to craft a message that is intended to be communicated in the most suitable manner towards the other party or parties involved in the communication process.

Please note as with any skill, mastering this technique requires practice. There will be many times you might fail, but the idea is to never give up and keep practicing until it becomes an automatic muscle that works in your favor.

We cannot prevent all the negativity that is happening around us. However, if we are conscious about our thoughts, words, and actions, we can absolutely prevent creating negativity that ultimately destroys ourselves.

"You can't change how people treat you or what they say about you. All you can do is change how you react to it." - Mahatma Gandhi

CONFLICTS IN RELATIONSHIPS

Have you played tug-of-war in your daily life?

Tug-of-war is a contest in which 2 teams pull at opposite ends of a rope until one drags the other over a central line.

We may not be playing this game physically with the people around us; however, mentally we all go through a tug-of-war with different kinds of people around us. Sometimes it is between nations, sometimes it is between religions, sometimes it is between different beliefs. Most often these kinds of tugs-of-war, which are usually for power, position, wealth, or fame, impact our lives negatively, causing pain and suffering. We deal with conflicts every day in our life. Conflicts can be constructive or destructive. Be it at school, the workplace, home, or even outdoors. We may not be able to solve all the conflicts in the world. However, is there a solution to resolve conflicts that happen in our daily lives?

The 4 simple conflict resolution strategies that we can apply in our daily lives to be happier and more peaceful in life are:

Strategy 1: Self-Awareness

This involves coming to awareness of the negative emotional states in a conflict. It emerges due to perceived differences between parties or for gaining control of the other party.

As an example, part of my role in my workplace is finding defects in the product and reporting them to the team, which includes developers who work hard to implement their ideas into the product. This process involves pointing to the problems with the code that impact the product. Being self-aware during such situations has helped me to stay calm and accept that negative impacts could arise from reporting the problems. After becoming self-aware, the next strategy involves self-preparation.

Strategy 2: Self-Preparation

Self-preparation involves taking complete responsibility for your emotional state and understanding that you own your emotions rather than believing others' behaviors affect your emotions. The key to doing this is to look at the conflict in an objective way by separating people from the problem. People have feelings and need to be treated as human beings but understanding through compassion that they are not the problem can help us disassociate the problem from the people.

To give an example—in my workplace, I had a coworker who always considered me as a competitor and would oppose everything that was presented by me. It was initially hard for me to deal with conflicts when I took the problems personally. However, when I started responding by taking charge of my emotions and looking at solving the problem rather than the person, I was able to respond positively and effectively.

Having made self-preparation, the next stage is conflict reduction.

Strategy 3: Conflict Reduction

Conflict reduction involves applying reflective listening capabilities to listen to the other person's view point, clarifying your understanding, and then sharing your own view point. This process helps to clarify similarities and differences in opinion. In a particular instance, during a team meeting, the same coworker who considered me as a competitor, blamed me for taking more time to complete a task that he believed was causing a delay in product delivery. I listened to him completely without being emotional. This helped me to understand the reason for his concern and deliver my response with facts and numbers that helped him to understand my part of reality and apologize for the blame.

The last stage in the conflict resolution process is called the negotiation phase.

Strategy 4: Negotiation Phase

The negotiation phase involves arriving at a mutually acceptable solution that satisfies both the parties. This process requires applying a problem-solving mindset to help arrive at a solution that helps solve the problem in an amicable manner. The general interest of both parties plays a major role in determining the solution. In the previous example with my coworker, both of our intentions were to maintain and improve product quality, but the aspects that were looked at were from different perspectives. Arriving at an agreement by highlighting the general interest of both parties can help you arrive at the solution faster and resolve conflicts.

As there are many types of minds in this world, there are as many different personalities who have their own shortcomings that are the result of upbringing, environment, and many other uncontrollable factors. By being self-aware, prepared, using active listening, and problem-solving we can resolve conflicts in our lives to an extent by letting go of our ego and collaborating with compassion. Problems exist in our minds and not in people.

REFLECTION

1. What are the relationship conflicts that have been causing you emotional pain?
2. When do you find yourself compromising your identity in your relationship?
3. What changes can you bring in your communication style to retain your identity in your relationship?

CHAPTER 17

APPLYING ANCIENT WISDOM

SELF-RELIANCE

"Do we not realize that self-respect comes from self-reliance?"
- A. P. J. Abdul Kalam

HOW CAN WE DISCOVER INTERNAL freedom and mental strength to endure challenges in life?

The magical key to the house of freedom is self-reliance or self-sufficiency. Self-reliance is the ability to tap into one's internal strength to face life's challenges and adversities. It is an internal mental state where you are happy and content with deep faith in yourself, experiencing completeness regardless of the changing people and situations around us. There are numerous great leaders, poets, thinkers, and social reformers who have lived and are living in today's world, achieving huge success using this power of self-reliance. Have you heard of the musk deer that produces scented fragrance? Musk deer is one of the most endangered species in the world. They have a special gland that produces a beautiful fragrance. However, the deer does not know where the smell comes from, and it looks around outside itself for the source of the beautiful smell.

Just like the musk deer, all of us are born with incredible power within us that is derived from the universe and is the source of strength, freedom, and happiness.

However, many of us never get a chance to realize or experience this power due to the walls within our internal environment created from upbringing, limited thinking, past memories, beliefs, and more. To realize this power and become self-reliant, it is important to be ready to unlearn, relearn, and reprogram our thinking, actions, and behavior so that we can utilize our internal resources most effectively to live a fulfilled life. It's not too late to restart your journey when you notice that your life is constantly going through ups and downs of sorrow, suffering, and discontent.

SELF-DISCOVERY

"Self-discovery is the beginning of all wisdom." - Aristotle

In the second chapter, we looked at different human needs that we all seek in our life. Once we have satisfied the basic external needs, it is important to satisfy our internal needs for our self-development so that we can move towards self-actualization. One of the most important attributes that we will notice when we are closer to self-actualization is self-sufficiency or self-reliance.

Each one of us is sent to this beautiful planet for a unique purpose. Whether we realize it or not, we all have the internal resources to lead a happy and peaceful life. Remember the time when you were a baby. If you don't remember, look at a six-month-old baby's face. They always live in joy unless they are hungry or in pain. It is only when they are in need of food or in pain or discomfort that they reach out to adults. Similarly, we all have immense potential within us that has the power to enable us to solve our own problems, make our own decisions, and live a life of freedom when we begin to untangle ourselves from the chains of past beliefs and perceptions by developing our mental strength through self-reliance, which takes us eventually to resilience. Unless we develop resilience, we will always keep complaining, blaming, resenting, and going through various emotional sufferings that prevent us from leading a life of joy and freedom.

Like how a laptop or mobile is programmed, created, and functions in a particular manner, we all have been created with our physical body, mind, and soul. When our internal and external resources function appropriately, we derive the maximum results. The internal resources that we all have in our possession include our mindset, emotional intelligence, values, attitude, and habits in combination with our inner wisdom. Self-reliance is the ability to use your internal resources effectively. It means believing in yourself even when the whole world refuses to believe in you. Every human being can become self-reliant in their lives. Self-discovery is the process that takes us towards realizing our true potential and living as our higher self, tuned to divine intelligence.

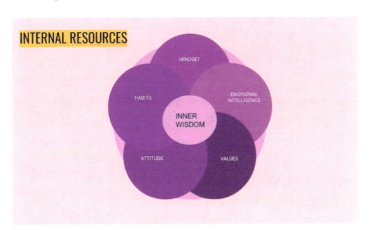

It is when we do not know who we are that we get distracted by various internal and external noises around us. The internal noises are our own negative self-critical voices that show up in the form of self-doubt or negative thinking, preventing us from leading a life of freedom. The external noises can take the form of influences from our closer circle, which includes our family, friends, peers, and more.

By setting boundaries, detaching, and self-regulating, these internal and external noises can be reduced by using the tools and techniques shared in the previous chapters. After having done that, the mind begins to listen to you as a student to a teacher and will show you the direction towards the inner voice, which some of us occasionally experience through intuition. It is otherwise called the "gut feeling." When we begin trusting that little divine voice and live by it, self-belief develops to a place of no fear about anyone or anything in this world. If you have controlled your mind, your world of joy or sorrow is in your control.

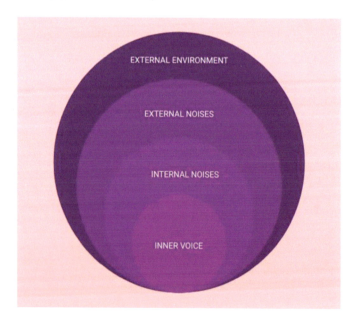

Self-discovery does not mean you have to give up your duties as a householder or give up your profession. It only means understanding your true self who is beyond the thoughts or emotions. This true self hidden in all of us is the spark of higher intelligence. When we break the walls of our beliefs, cleanse our internal mental world, and cultivate positivity the authentic self speaks through us.

IDENTITY

We all form identity about ourselves right from our childhood. Our identity is our perception of ourself and is shaped based on our past, environment, values, likes and dislikes, and beliefs about ourselves in this world. We may project some of our identity through physical self-image before others. The actual you is not the one you see in the mirror. Behind the body is a shining higher self that is covered by the mind. Self-actualization described in Maslow's hierarchy of needs and Moksha, mentioned in the Purushartha, refers to realizing the higher self who has infinite potential.

The unique values that we possess and consider most important in our lives are what we project in our relationships and at work. These values are our strengths that build our character. When we compromise our values, we are compromising ourselves, which leads to dissatisfaction and unhappiness. Eventually, this leads to losing ourselves and living the identity of others. Our true identity is the identity of our higher self. As discussed in the previous chapter, when you become a Sthithaprajna, one who is resilient internally, you begin to exhibit the qualities of the higher self. These qualities include being courageous, balanced, compassionate, vigilant, selfless in serving the world, and rational.

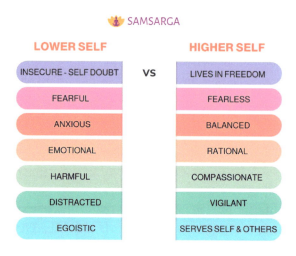

SAMSARGA

LOWER SELF		HIGHER SELF
INSECURE - SELF DOUBT	VS	LIVES IN FREEDOM
FEARFUL		FEARLESS
ANXIOUS		BALANCED
EMOTIONAL		RATIONAL
HARMFUL		COMPASSIONATE
DISTRACTED		VIGILANT
EGOISTIC		SERVES SELF & OTHERS

We are all innately pure in nature. When we are under the control of our mind through our strong beliefs, thoughts, and emotions, we project our lower self that leads to pain and suffering. When we carry out our actions and behave in identification to our higher self, we not only become positive and happier but also act from a place of our true identity as the higher self. A simple way to live as your higher self is to remind yourself every time you fall into the trap of the lower self that you are not the lower self but the higher self who has powerful attributes, and bring yourself consciously back to your balance. This state of higher self is the natural state where you feel, think, and act authentically. I have found that when I act from a place of higher self, I am grounded, present, energetic, creative, productive, and efficient because the lower self is no longer in charge. Being in the zone of the higher self has also enabled me to allow intuition and inner wisdom to flow to offer the right advice and guidance to people in need of it. You then become open to the higher intelligence flowing through you.

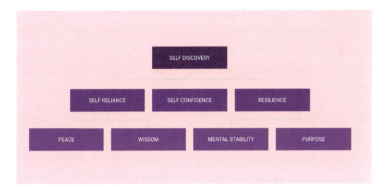

Among the various attributes that one develops during self-discovery is self-confidence, which is the most common ingredient that many of us lack when we get to places of self-doubt and other forms of emotional pain. We usually assess our worth based on the respect, recognition, or value that others place on us. We place our worthiness on external factors like self-image, social status, wealth, jobs, relationships, and more. Although these are related to us, our worth does not lie in these factors. Our worth lies in the unique strengths and abilities that we are gifted in this world.

Self-confidence is based on the belief in our worth.

My self-worth or esteem was challenged from a very small age. I believed I was not good enough based on the negative criticism that I received as I grew up. This belief prevented me from speaking up and being my authentic self in various situations in my life. When I became an adult, the belief followed, and I began noticing I was holding myself back in my workplace and various social situations. I felt disappointed in myself for not being able to stand up, advocate, and share my voice in front of others. I relied on external approval for carrying out my tasks. Decision-making was hard for me as I was afraid of making mistakes.

Developing confidence occurred in stages for me. I had to challenge myself to get out of my comfort zone every time that little voice in my head said, "Don't do it." As I began slowly moving out of my comfort zone, my belief in myself grew. Along with this, I began spending more time with positive people who encouraged and uplifted me. The amazing support from my mother, who is my role model in my life, along with the support from my teachers, coaches, and mentors, pushed me to take extraordinary actions. The amazing resources gifted to me led me to take extraordinary actions that brought outstanding results in my life. This eventually increased my belief in myself. This included creating online courses in Sanskrit that taught nearly 10,000 students across 139 countries, launching my podcast *The Peace Bridge*, becoming the host of *The Peace Bridge Podcast* on VoiceAmerica, and more. Each time I accomplished a goal, it proved my worth for me. It made me reflect on my unique abilities and the value they brought to the projects and people with whom I worked. Each time I performed an action that challenged my self-doubt, my confidence increased within me. The feeling of not being enough made me take actions to feel enough and ultimately discover my life's purpose as coaching. This eventually led me to develop self-acceptance, forgiveness, and self-love within myself.

I discovered my true calling in life was to inspire, educate, and empower people around me. As I began filling the cup of others and serving with my heart, I began living my purpose through coaching people with emotional pain, and my self-worth bumped up very high. The biggest realization that I had was that I am beyond the limitations of my body and mind as I was created by a higher intelligence. I am complete and enough regardless of what I do and what I don't do.

I am grateful to the divine power for molding me into who I am today where I can share the divine wisdom through my voice. You don't have to be like anyone else. You just have to be authentically you. You are the creator of your destiny. When you believe in yourself, the rest of the world will follow you. There is only one you, so don't give up on yourself. In the Holy Bhagavad Gita, Lord Krishna says when you abuse yourself, you are abusing the spark of himself in you.

Apply the following strategies to live a worthy life:

1. **Acknowledge your strengths**—Our strengths are unique to ourselves and build our personality. When we focus on our strengths, recognize, and utilize them, we will be able to increase our self-worth, making us feel proud of ourselves. Use your strengths to help someone around you.

2. **Live by your values every day**—Each one of us has different values in life. When we live by our values, we feel much more satisfied and content from within. Pick 3 values that are most important in your life, and try using them every day to develop a positive attitude.

3. **Practice self-love**—Self-love means falling in love with yourself regardless of your weakness and imperfections. By accepting yourself as you are with love, you become kind to yourself. Developing self-love is important to be able to stand up for yourself and feel important.

4. **Entertain positive self-talk**—The stories that we tell ourselves each day make us who we are. So be mindful of your self-talk, and keep it positive so that you are rewarded by building up your self-worth.

"Stay true to yourself. An original is worth more than a copy." - Suzy Kassem

Take charge of yourself now, before you lose yourself with time. Let's all take the responsibility to reconstruct ourselves as stronger and healthier humans who are a boon to the community and the world.

SELF-AWARENESS

Having self-awareness means being conscious of your own thoughts, emotions, and actions.

Why is it important to be self-aware? When we are not self-aware, our attention is always focused on the external world and fixing it to gain control of our peace and happiness. When we are unaware, we place the disturbances in our mind in the form of envy, hatred, anger, and jealousy onto someone else to satisfy our emotional thirst. However, we all know from our own personal experiences that this will not shut off the fire but will aggravate it in many forms, leading to conflicts, wars, communal issues, and more. The beliefs in our mind that make up our thoughts and actions are what lead this to happen. It is only when we turn within us, by developing self-awareness, that we will be able to notice that there is a mess inside of us that needs to be cleaned, which has been causing harm to ourselves and to others.

Self-introspection is what enabled me to reflect on my behavior and take action towards developing self-awareness. In the beginning of my journey to discover peace, I believed my thoughts and used to be reactive to people and situations in my life. Whatever I threw out as anger or worry or fear came back to me and caused me pain. So I began thinking deeply on whether there were other ways to solve my problems. This is when I learned and integrated mindfulness into my life by becoming aware of my thoughts, emotions, and actions. I noticed that I was reacting to situations when I was unconscious, especially in my family and work environment.

I experimented with becoming more aware of my triggers, my weaknesses, and everything that took me to emotional pain. As I became more and more aware, I noticed that I was not leaving my balanced state of mind unless I became unconscious. This alertness that is developed from awareness is a natural quality inherent in us, which we have begun losing due to the enormous distractions in and around us. Although we claim that we are the most highly evolved beings, if we watch animals, we will notice that they are much more aware than us.

This may sound funny. One of the ways that helped me understand the value of awareness was by watching my cat, Peaches. She is always aware of the smallest sounds and familiar sights, even when she is sleeping. This has always amazed me. She is disciplined and sweet, but she is always on alert mode, on guard, and fully focused and prepared even when she pretends to sit idle in the corner of the couch. There are many ways to develop self-awareness. An effective process that has worked for me is using mantras to do a practice called Japa, which means repeated chanting of the mantra while being conscious of the sound and meaning of the mantra. This powerful practice not only improves your awareness but also develops focus and memory and brings positivity into your life.

SELF-CONTROL

We all live on a planet among living and nonliving beings. How are we humans different from others among all the living beings that exist? The human brain is the most evolved among all the living creatures on this beautiful planet. The most important distinguishing factor that we, as humans, possess is the ability to think and use the power of discrimination. This power of discrimination helps us to think clearly, make decisions, and act sensibly. All of us are born with good and bad tendencies inherited and accumulated from our past. These can impact our behavior through our thoughts, feelings, and actions. When we lead an unconscious life, we become trapped in our lower tendencies and act based on that, eventually preventing our ability to think clearly, discriminate, and behave accordingly. In our modern world, we all encounter various challenges at work, in relationships, in family, with children, and more. When we cannot solve the challenges ourselves, we resort to external objects around us to provide seemingly quick temporary fixes.

These quick fixes could be social media, devices, smoking, alcohol, drugs, substances, and more. When the dependency on any of these sources goes beyond moderation, we fall into the trap of addictions. When we are under the control of our habits, we lose our unique ability to think clearly, make accurate decisions, and behave appropriately.

Since the time of COVID-19, there has been a rapid increase in the rise of abuse of and mental health issues due to addictions. Any substitution through external objects will not provide a lasting solution to our problems; instead, it will degrade our evolved brains to a pathetic state of human degeneration.

We can all rise above our lower tendencies by developing self-discipline and self-control. Self-control does not mean suppressing our feelings or thoughts and acting the best before others. Self-control means developing an internal discipline of training the mind by managing our thoughts and emotions effectively to live a peaceful and happy life. In the Holy Bhagavad Gita, Lord Krishna mentions to Arjuna that such a person who controls his senses is a man of perfection with steady wisdom.

We create our mental dependencies in life, but we can all rise above them if we develop self-control. Through self-control, we will be able to conserve our energy and direct it towards a noble vision that will not only uplift our mindset, bring us peace, and take us to the best version of ourselves but also contribute towards protecting humanity.

MEDITATION

Now, let's try this simple meditation.

Please do not carry out this meditation while you are driving.

- Close your eyes.
- Sit straight with your back erect.
- Focus your attention on the middle of your chest.
- Imagine you are sitting on a river shore.
- There is a fresh breeze, the sound of the river is ringing in your ears, and the color of the river is sky blue.
- Sitting on the river shore, you watch the river flowing in a rhythm.
- Everything looks so quiet and perfect.
- Now you find a leaf next to you. Visualize one addiction you are ready to release, and place it on the leaf.
- Then, place the leaf on the flowing water. The river carries the leaf from the place you left it, slowly and steadily, until it vanishes from your sight.
- You then fold your hands together and thank the universe for supporting you to help eliminate your addiction.
- With deep gratitude, slowly open your eyes.

SELF-LOVE

We run around looking for love, recognition, and acceptance everywhere. Many people firmly believe that happiness can be achieved only when everything around us is perfect and everyone loves us and lives according to our expectations. We look for acceptance and validation from everyone around us to progress in life and consider that we can be successful, happy, and content if we receive it. We often prioritize everyone around us to please and make everyone happy for our happiness. However, we hardly have time to enjoy our company. Each of us is created as unique individuals with immense potential to live a life of happiness if we permit ourselves.

BEFORE COACHING

Tania was a very well organized, intelligent, selfless, and capable single woman. She brought up her children and took care of her parents flawlessly. Her daily schedule involved cooking and taking care of the family. She put her family's needs before her needs. She did not get a break from her lifestyle and felt burned out by the end of the day after carrying out all the responsibilities on her shoulders. The last person that she took care of was herself. She pleased everyone around her so that they would love and respect her unconditionally. Eventually, she noticed that others around her took her service for granted and did not return the love she offered them.

This grew discontent, frustration, and anger inside her and made her feel unwanted. When Tania came for the coaching sessions, she wanted to find a way to advance spiritually to overcome the emotional pain she was going through in her life.

As a step towards that, I asked if she loved herself, and she said no. She said she hated her appearance and certain qualities in her. We went through a short meditation to help her forgive herself and fall in love with herself. As she went through this process, she had unexplainable joy. She later told me she had always ignored herself and never paid attention to her own needs.

AFTER COACHING

As Tania began loving herself deeply, she was able to prioritize her needs and started becoming vocal about her opinions. She derived unshakeable courage and wisdom that eventually helped her to share the love within her with the people around her. She no longer complained that nobody wanted her. Instead, she began following her heart and carrying out tasks that brought more profound meaning to her life. Tania is now a busy woman working on her book that will be published in a few months.

WAYS TO PRACTICE SELF-LOVE

1. Dedicate some time in your day to enjoy your own company, which nobody can provide you even if they try their best.
2. Love and accept yourself for who you are based on your values.
3. Acknowledge yourself for your efforts.
4. Celebrate your achievements.
5. Forgive yourself for your mistakes.

If you enjoy your own company, you will stop looking for someone else to make you happy. Happiness is a state that is not dependent on the external environment but dependent on your internal environment. Developing your internal environment is the only way to lasting peace and happiness. Spend time and energy working on yourself rather than chasing the world and waiting for it to grant peace and happiness to you.

REFLECTION

1. On a scale of 0–10 (0 being lowest, 10 being highest), how much do you love yourself?
2. What activities do you carry out in your day to love yourself?
3. How would your life change if you loved yourself deeply?

SELF-MOTIVATION

Have you been tired of relying on external resources to motivate you?

Most of us look for external sources of motivation in the form of books, podcasts, and people. While they help to motivate us, they only replace self-motivation once we achieve our goals in life. When we perform our everyday tasks lacking motivation, our work becomes uninteresting and does not help us grow.

Self-motivation has lots of benefits. Some include promoting a positive attitude and improving self-esteem, self-resilience, independence, freedom, courage, and inner contentment. How can we self-motivate ourselves regardless of our situations or external validations? These 4 simple steps can help us be self-motivated so that we can continue to accomplish our goals regardless of whether we are rewarded.

1. **Reason**—Finding the "why" behind our actions can give us clarity and insight into the purpose of doing the task with more focused attention. This can also help us better understand the

benefits of performing a task at hand. For example, driving was not my passion, so getting a driver's license was not something I was deeply motivated to do for a long time. However, by looking at the benefits that driving could provide to me and my family, it encouraged me to learn and upgrade my skills, which eventually enabled me to receive my driver's license.

2. **Energy**—Create an internal loving connection with the activity by making it as fun as possible. For example, ask questions such as, "How can I make this experience enjoyable rather than boring?" In terms of driving, I developed a connection with my car by looking at it not as a mere vehicle but as my good friend and then considering those moments of driving as good times with a good friend who was taking me to different destinations.

3. **Connection**—Surround yourself with people who can uplift your spirit, challenge you, and move you out of your comfort zone, which includes mentors, teachers, coaches, spiritual guides, etc. For example, the driving challenges provided by my driving coach helped me move out of my comfort zone and take up challenging driving tasks that motivated me to work hard and gain my driver's license.

4. **Reward**—Celebrate every small win you make in your progress to accomplish your goal. This is an acknowledgment to yourself and will give you the fuel to take up similar tasks and make it happen.

As you carry out these 4 steps, you will notice that you feel contented and fulfilled regardless of the outcome or result the action will generate.

By developing internal motivation, we focus on the process rather than the outcome. This way, we can enjoy our work by putting ourselves entirely into it and living in the present rather than becoming anxious about the results.

The Holy Bhagavad Gita states:

कर्मण्येवाधिकारस्ते मा फलेषु कदाचन।
मा कर्मफलहेतुर्भूर्मा ते सङ्गोऽस्त्वकर्मणि।।

Karmanyeva Adhikaraste ma phaleshu kadachana
Ma karma phala hetur bhur ma te sanghostu akarmani

"You have the right to work only but not on the results. Let neither the results of action be your motive nor let your attachment be to inaction."[30]

BEFORE COACHING

Jerry was a research scientist. She was intelligent and educated. However, the projects that were assigned to her seemed like they needed to be easier for her. She did not have the motivation to work on her projects to complete them on time. This caused frustration, agitation, and disappointment in her. She could not get help from her friends as they were also in similar situations and did not know how to help her.

Jerry approached me, and we began working on her problem of lack of motivation. During the coaching session, Jerry mentioned that she could not innovate or have the creative ideas required for presenting research papers. Her day was occupied with finding solutions to certain formulas and pieces of code that were not working. Her instructors also needed to gain the technical knowledge to support her. It required her to develop

---

30   The Holy Bhagavad Gita 2:47

self-motivation to complete the projects on time and with the highest quality.

So as we went through the session, I enabled her to set mini goals for her project that were achievable in a short period, along with building a solid schedule that included self-care time and rewarding herself every time she reached a milestone. When she put this into practice, she noticed that the failures from each experiment discouraged her from moving forward. So we had to change her perspective on failure by detaching herself from it, viewing it as feedback, and applying possible alternatives available to her.

AFTER COACHING

After implementing all these strategies, Jerry completed her project and presented it confidently before the board, which later led to her being chosen as one of the students to travel abroad for a conference.

REFLECTION

1. What motivation are you missing out on in your life?
2. When do you feel a lack of motivation?
3. How can you motivate yourself to carry out the task before you?

DETACHMENT

Detachment does not mean giving up everything and everyone in your life and living in sorrow. Detachment means being able to see our relationships without attachment to your own. Attachment arises from our ego, and when clouded with ego, we expect people around us to behave in a way that matches our expectations. Most often, in our daily relationships at home, we get into places of attachment that eventually lead to various problems. There is attachment towards our partner, attachment towards children, attachment towards work, attachment towards money, and more. When we look closely, wherever there is attachment, there is also sorrow. The attachment styles that we all have in our relationships are derived from our beliefs, culture, and learnings from our surroundings.

For example, when we get married, we form an attachment towards our partner; when we have a newborn child, we have an attachment towards our children. As soon as we form these attachments, we are tying ourselves to the person in the form of mental dependencies. When these mental dependencies are unmet for some reason, we become disappointed. However, these mental dependencies are our creations that can be changed at our will through the power of detachment.

Four common attachment styles seen in relationships are:

- **Anxious**—This style seeks partner approval, support, and responsiveness.
- **Avoidant**—People who use this style don't want to depend on others or have others rely on them.
- **Fearful**—This style means acting from a place of fear of getting hurt and having trouble trusting.
- **Secure**—This style represents positive support, respect, and connection with each other.

The way we interact within our relationships is based on the attachment style. The most common style that arises from self-doubt includes the anxious and fearful style. When we continue following this pattern, we degrade our relationships and ourselves.

We project this attachment style into our marriages, parenting, workplace relationships, and more. This eventually leads to developing unhealthy relationships that disturb the environment around us and lead to separation. An anxious attachment style eventually leads to codependency in relationships, lower self-esteem, and more.

In our relationships, conflicts begin to arise when each person brings in a particular attachment style derived from their upbringing, beliefs, or culture. It is possible to bring in a secure attachment style that allows growth for both people involved in the relationship by recognizing the unhealthy state of the relationship and taking action as individuals to fix ourselves before fixing our relationships.

Our attachments form unrealistic expectations in our relationships; when unmet, we become frustrated, agitated, and discontented. My marriage was an arranged marriage. I started knowing about my husband only once we started living under the same roof. We began our married life with lots of dreams, hopes, and expectations. Our perceptions and beliefs about our partners before the marriage matched regarding looks, family, jobs, and social status, but our perceptions about our personalities differed in our minds.

We began our lives together. The first few months went by happily as a perfect couple, but as months progressed, we started noticing conflicting habits, attitudes, and behaviors in different situations. I followed my husband's decisions blindly as I was told to be very obedient and listen to my spouse's decisions and opinions. This belief was mine and was not imposed by my spouse.

I didn't realize I was compromising myself, pleasing my spouse, and agreeing to everything without sharing my voice. I considered myself lower than my spouse and became codependent to the extent that I looked for validation for whether to do the smallest activity or not. Self-doubt increased as I continued to do this again and again. I became stuck and helpless.

One day, my spouse told me, "You are well educated and talented, but you act like an elephant that does not know its size." I began profoundly reflecting on his response, and that gave me the confirmation that I have everything in me, and seeking out validation was due to my lack of belief in myself.

As soon as I heard this statement, I realized I had created this mental dependency on my spouse from my attachment. Marriage is built on values of love, trust, respect, and acceptance. It is different for everyone. However, it does not mean giving up your identity for your values. My relationship flourished when I began believing in my values and expressing my identity.

My relationship grew from anxious attachment to a secure attachment style when I began integrating mindfulness into my communication, developing acceptance and gratitude, incorporating personal time into my schedule, and establishing boundaries. As I followed this approach, I slowly moved from anxiety to a place where I was no longer mentally dependent and expressed my authentic self. Our relationship broke the ties of attachment and moved to a style with more understanding, respect, love, and trust that grew out of emotional maturity rather than expectations. This created more freedom in both our lives and has allowed us to be ourselves in our relationship without compromising our values while being in our relationship.

In such a relationship, nobody is controlling the other person. We allow the other person to be who they are without bringing in our expectations, past, or negative beliefs about the person. You are looking at the person as they are at the moment.

Detachment brings peace because we are no longer dependent on people or situations to be happy in our life. When we practice detachment, we see people as they are with their personalities. It then becomes easier for us to behave with the proper perspective.

REFLECTION

1. Which attachment style do you follow in your relationship?
2. Which areas of your relationship are causing you to follow this attachment style?
3. What would you change if you had the chance to change your relationship style?
4. How can the new relationship style change your life?

SELF-TALK

The stories we tell each day shape us into who we are every day of our lives. How we talk to ourselves is often not taught in schools or colleges, but if we lack this understanding, we fall into the trap of negative thinking. We can slowly teach positive self-talk by changing how we perceive information from the external world. Our experiences are based on our perceptions, and when we perceive positively, we change our experiences. Many of us are submerged in negative self-talk when we have negative perceptions of people and situations. These then enter our minds and cause disturbances that affect our emotions and behavior.

When we become aware through the indication provided by our emotions, we can slowly take a detour and bring about a state of balance and positivity through positive self-talk. Positive self-talk has served me the most as a powerful weapon during failures, rejections, negative criticism, and neglect. Being compassionate, I always took the smallest act of neglect when someone did not look at my face or recognize my presence very seriously. I used to believe that it was because something was wrong with me that people didn't acknowledge me and my worth. This belief used to eat at me for days, and I used to feel very bad about myself. I would go down the route of emotional self-harm and suffering.

One day, as I was about to sit and meditate, this discomfort brought me deep sorrow. I knew that meditating with this kind of mind would not get me anywhere. I told myself that I needed help in understanding how to stop dwelling on someone neglecting me. So I asked my friend—my mind—"Why does this person not acknowledge me?" My mind replied, "Maybe they don't know about you." I wondered to whom the problem belonged. My mind replied, "It is their problem." So I received my answer. If it is their problem that they don't know my worth, why do I have to waste my thinking and energy to prove myself to someone who doesn't like me as much as I do myself? This powerful insight cleared my mind and allowed me to meditate deeply. After the meditation, I returned to my centered state to continue performing the activity right before me with complete involvement.

Next time the same person who had neglected me did the same on a different occasion. Their neglect did not bother me, and I remained as I was, believing and being comfortable with myself. To my surprise, this person came down to me and asked my opinion on a place I was about to visit in India.

The best friend you have for yourself is your mind. It can help you find answers to your most profound problems if you purify it and listen to the whispers of the higher self that it communicates to you. You must be aware and listen to how you attend as though to a crying baby. Giving the crying baby whatever it needs will most likely make the baby become silent and allow you to do whatever you want. When the crying settles down, what remains is just peace.

Positive self-talk can also be cultivated through self-affirmative statements that begin with "I am." It is not enough to repeat these affirmations mechanically; the power lies in believing them as you state them. For example, "I am enough" is a powerful affirmation, but repeating "I am enough" 100 times will not make you enough. It is when you genuinely feel that you are sufficient that it re-instills positive energy within you to act in your daily life. I have listed below some of the powerful affirmations that have been helpful to me and my clients.

Examples of a few affirmations:

- I am enough.
- I am beautiful.
- I am kind.
- I am intelligent.
- I am lovable.
- I am valued.
- I am recognized.
- I am appreciated.
- I am talented.
- I am caring.
- I am respected.
- I am confident.
- I am truthful.

REFLECTION

1. What are the common self-talk statements that you experience in your daily life?
2. Which self-talk statements would you like to change?
3. What positive self-talk statements can you use to replace your existing ones?
4. How will this new self-talk benefit your life?

CHAPTER 18

CULTIVATING PEACE

"Peace will not come from the sky. Peace must be built through our own actions."

- His Holiness The Dalai Lama

WHAT IS PEACE?

Peace is freedom from our own internal chattering of the mind. This freedom that we are looking for outside us cannot be found through people or objects or situations. It is a treasure that needs to be explored within us. We can derive this peace when the mind becomes still and calm. This is attainable only through managing our senses that give rise to thoughts and emotions. Practicing mindfulness can help us to achieve this self-control through which we can remain in the present moment. Just like we can see pebbles on a placid lake, we will be able to see our true identity when we arrive at this peaceful state. This unshaken peace cannot be stolen by anyone and is attained when mind and heart become one. By directing our thoughts towards a higher purpose, we will be able to sustain this peace forever.

We no longer have to run away from anything in our life when we have the control of ourselves and our peace.

Among the Gunas that we looked at earlier, Satva is the Guna that brings in the state of peace, calmness, balance, and happiness that is filled with positivity. Satva represents the field with the highest energy that is the source of creativity and wisdom and connects us to higher intelligence. When the mind is purified and Satva arrives, it becomes blissful with conserved energy.

A person who has moved to Satva is one who has risen from the lower self and manifests qualities of the higher self. Such a person is the Sthithaprajna who has trained the mind to a place of peace and balance by being centered.

The resilient mindset of the Sthitaprajna makes them capable of facing external situations with ease, which do not affect them internally. The internal environment of the Sthithaprajna shields them from the external situation and enables them to rise above challenges as a warrior in life.

There could be times in life when we might slip and fall off this path. Instead of beating ourselves terribly, we can all rise back up and continue our journey towards Satva. The secret lies in recognizing through self-awareness which state we are currently in and taking action towards choosing the state in which we would like to be in order to reach Satva.

For example, when you are feeling sad or disappointed, if you are self-aware, you will notice that you are in a Tamas state which generates negative energy. Being in that state will not allow you to grow but instead will degrade you further.

After recognizing through awareness that you are in a state that is not the ideal state, notice the thoughts and emotions associated with that state without becoming involved in them as involvement will make you react based on your thoughts and emotions. When we begin separating ourselves from our thoughts and emotions, we will notice that negative thoughts and emotions take control over us when we give importance to them and believe them. They are like guests who come to our house. We don't entertain all the guests in our house. We only let those people in whom we know and trust. If we know they would cause us pain, we leave them at the door as much as possible.

We cannot change the people or situations around us to not cause painful events, but we can change the way we look at them by managing ourselves effectively. Each time we notice ourselves going down the path to Tamas or Rajas, it is important for us to take suitable actions to bring us back to the ideal energy state of Satva to maintain the peace and calm that will keep us happy. As we continue this practice diligently, we will understand that it is a matter of shifting ourselves with patience and choice. There could be good, bad, or neutral thoughts and emotions. Choosing any of them will color us and make us behave accordingly. Like an actor who wears the clothes of a king would act like a king, when we give in to the emotion of anger, we become an angry person and do things related to anger.

You are not your thoughts and emotions. You are the higher self whose nature is balanced, equanimous, and peaceful.

Your freedom and peace are within you. So don't look for the treasure outside. Purify your mind and peace will be yours.

Emotions are our guides that can show us our current emotional state. Instead of reacting based on them, we need to step into the role of a parent who takes care of a child who does not know what to do at times. When we intervene with the right intelligence, we will be able to guide each emotion back to the ideal state with consistent practice. Each tool within ancient wisdom is provided to help us arrive at this self-awareness and allow divinity to flow through us by purifying our mind so that we can live a life of peace and happiness anytime and anywhere in our life.

EQUANIMITY

Equanimity is a state where you have the same outlook towards good and bad, fortune and misfortune, failure and success, friend and enemy. This may sound strange as to how you can look at these opposite pairs in the same manner.

Well, when we think and act from a place of ego, we will not be able to look at everything around us in the same way. However, when we develop qualities of forgiveness, gratitude, and compassion towards others and situations, eventually we will notice that we cannot control or change anything.

It is the pride, prejudice, or bias in us that prevents us from looking at others as we are. These are created by us to satisfy our own egocentric desires. They may or may not be true. Whether true or not, it only causes disturbance in our mind, preventing us from behaving, talking, or acting authentically towards the other person. When this happens, we get into a place of creating further sorrow for others and ourselves. It is important to understand that pretending that we are good externally and then carrying jealousy, greed, and hatred will only weigh us down to our lower self.

This applies to various events or situations in our life, too. When we experience failure, we may become dejected and believe that something is wrong with us and that is why we failed. If we are in this state, we will not be able to move forward. However, if we detach ourselves from the results of our actions, we will be able to find alternative ways to solve it rather than personalizing it. This approach will give us a way to look at both success and failure as the same.

When it comes to people, everybody has the 3 qualities of Tamas, Rajas, and Satva, and we act based on them differently. However, the true self that resides in all of us is the same. When we label someone as our enemy, this does not change the true self residing in them. It is our projection that becomes our belief. Rather than holding to strong beliefs, if we forgive and let go, focusing on our path, we will be able to develop equanimity that allows us to face challenging situations courageously as everything that we need is in us.

I have found the practice of equanimity to work profoundly in my workplace when I had challenging personalities to work with. These personalities were extraordinary leaders and at the same time very rigid and egoistic in nature. Whenever I brought in a suggestion or ideas, they would blindly oppose it. Initially, it used to be very hard for me to work with them, and there were days when I almost went to the point of believing that they were stronger than me.

I began applying strategies to be like them—being loud and aggressive—but that did not help as it became like a fun movie for others to watch and did not improve anything.

So I began reflecting deeply and also consulted my mentors and coaches about it. I understood that these people were different in terms of their views, likes, dislikes, thinking, and more. As I deeply reflected, I understood that their ego was arising from fear that I would highlight their faulty areas, which could ruin their reputation.

When I understood this, I decided I should change my approach and look at them from a place of compassion. When I began approaching conversations with them from a place of compassion and love, they slowly began reflecting the same back to me. Every time I started the conversation, I would talk to them as though I was meeting them for the first time in my life, forgiving all that they had done to me before and understanding that they were also a work in progress just like me. Giving them the space to be themselves and believing that they were just like me who have amazing talents, made it easier for me to break the barriers of the differences between us. In spite of our differences, we have been able to build a relationship of love and trust rather than one with ego, competition, and hatred towards each other.

BALANCE

A balanced state of mind is one where the mind is settled in peace and no longer falls into the extremes of high excitement or deepest sorrow. The Satva state represents balance. One who is a Sthithaprajna exhibits this emotional state where there is steadiness exhibited at all times through their thoughts, emotions, and behavior.

This state is also when all the energies are aligned and centered. The grounded state is unshakeable and allows you to tap into your highest potential. The mind is no longer agitated and remains calm. Mind, body, and intelligence work in coordination beautifully. Therefore, you will be able to think clearly and rationally, be in control of yourself, and thus, can perform at your highest level. Being balanced can reduce our stress, increase our productivity and creativity, and bring deeper fulfillment and happiness into our lives.

This natural state of relaxation can be attained by bringing into our lives the following practices whenever we notice our mind getting into a place of agitation.

1. Silence
2. Reflection
3. Mindfulness
4. Self-control
5. Selfless service

6. Controlled breathing

It is important to note that only when all the basic human needs mentioned in Chapter 2 (Maslow's hierarchy) are satisfied that a mind can incorporate the above practices to develop balance. As each person in the world is different, the way each achieves balance is also different.

I have found these practices help me to bring me back to balance whenever my mind is agitated. In this state of balance one is highly energetic, innovative, productive, creative, and vibrant. Resetting back to the balanced state during energy depletion can be done anytime you feel exhausted and will provide you momentum to do more. This is because the mind is focused, and with the conserved energy, tasks can be carried out in a short period of time with highest efficiency.

STABILITY

The thoughts that run in our mind keep changing every moment. Many of us know what the instability of the mind looks like with the emotional distress caused by states of confusion, restlessness, frustration, anger, anxiety, overthinking, dejection, and disappointment. While being in an unstable state of mind, it becomes very difficult to push ourselves through our day to carry out our work and take care of our family in the best way. Our energies are drained, and we are stressed and exhausted most of the time. We discussed the 3 Gunas that we all possess in the previous chapters and how they can influence our state of mind. For example, when influenced by the Tamas Guna, we may have thoughts of unworthiness, inaction, and disappointment, which represent an unstable mind. In order to move into a stable state of mind, the essential qualities of Satva Guna should be cultivated. Before it becomes a natural state for the mind, it needs to be consciously cultivated through incorporating positive thoughts and actions throughout the day.

Some of the attributes of a stable mind are:

1. Ability to cope with challenges during the day
2. Ability to manage yourself and your relationships
3. Ability to think clearly and realistically
4. Ability to have high focus and energy
5. Being resilient

The same practices that we have discussed throughout the book help us to achieve stability through developing the mental disciplines of self-control, detachment, self-love, devotion, and reflection.

CHAPTER 19

SIXTEEN DAILY PRACTICES TO DISCOVER PEACE

1. **Meditation**

    *"Correct your mind and the rest of your
    life will fall into place."*

    - Lao Tzu

Meditation means giving love and attention to ourselves in order to tap the infinite potential of our minds. Meditation can help us to create inner peace and joy, which prepares us to stay calm as we encounter the challenges of the day. Taking a few minutes during your day to be with yourself and choosing a meditation that suits your mind can help start your day with the right mental clarity and focus. There are various forms of meditations, based on the nature of your mind, that we can incorporate, including mantra meditation, visualization, breathing meditation, Reiki healing meditation, and more.

What is your favorite meditation that you would like to start incorporating into your day?

2. **Positive mindset**

   The next practice is incorporating a positive mindset into your daily life.

   This means entertaining positive thoughts as much as possible even in the worst circumstances.

   We cannot control the minds of everyone that we interact with on a regular basis, but we can manage our thoughts and feelings by making them as clean as possible through positive thoughts. This will not only help us develop a growth mindset but will also change the atmosphere around us through our interactions.

   What is a positive thought that you would like to incorporate when you begin your day?

   _____

3. **Mindfulness**

   This is the act of living in the present moment. This means being mindful of every moment in your life, paying complete attention, and not becoming caught up in your past or future.

   Mindfulness can be practiced anytime and anywhere. I have found mindfulness helps me stay focused on my present moment, and I utilize it by focusing completely on the activity at hand. This activity not only helps to train our mind to improve our focus but also helps us to observe and respond to situations around us rather than reacting spontaneously.

I practice it every day and have seen profound benefits of protecting myself from negative experiences 90% of the time.

Just for today, what will you be mindful of?

_____

4. **Self-love**

Self-love is the ability to accept yourself as you are. It also means being able to forgive yourself for your mistakes and includes acknowledging your smallest achievements in life. We often seek validation from everyone around us but forget to love ourselves. If we don't love ourselves, we will continue to please others, believing that somebody else needs to make us happy. However, if we love ourselves, we will be able to act more confidently as our authentic selves.

Write 3 things that you love about yourself:

_____

_____

_____

5. **Gratitude**

Gratitude is one of the best ways to tackle negative thinking. It is one of the practices that helps our brain to shift to a positive mindset.

When we shift our focus towards what we are grateful for in life, we will complain less about things we do not have and continue to look at what we do have in our life. Try reminding yourself of 3 things that you are grateful for in your life and notice how you feel inside your mind.

I am grateful for:

_____

_____

_____

6. **Self-reflection**

Choose a place inside your home where you are comfortable and away from external disturbances. Sit silently, watch your breath, and pay complete attention to yourself for a few minutes. Look at your regular day, and dedicate some time for self-reflection.

Ask yourself these questions:

o   How did my day go?

_____

o   Where can I bring in change so that I can improve my tomorrow?

_____

o   What did I learn today about myself?

_____

o   How did I behave towards others?

_____

o   How did I respond to conversations?

_____

o   Pick one behavior or attitude that you believe will improve your tomorrow.

_____

If you believe you need assistance to bring change, then connect with a coach, mentor, or therapist to help you bring change into your life.

7. **Detox**

Take some time every day to detox your mind by disengaging from the digital world. This means giving yourself time to refrain from digital devices that include TV, laptop, mobile devices, etc. Allocate a time in your day to detox your mind and body from devices around you so that you can utilize your mind for non-digital activities that can include time for your passions or time to connect with your family and friends in person.

What will you use your detox time for?

_____

8. **Connect with nature**

Nature is the biggest healer in this world, and spending time in nature, as many of us know, can bring amazing health benefits. Allocate time during your day to be with nature and appreciate the beauty of nature. Go for short walks or bike rides, and notice how your mind and body feels refreshed with positive energy even after a short connection with nature.

Which time during the day will you spend time with nature?

_____

9. **Healthy connections**

Healthy connections can be any authentic connection with people, animals, books, or any media that gives you an opportunity to learn and grow. When we have the right people who can teach, guide, and empower us through their connections it can help us uplift our mindset and provide us with positive energy. So dedicate a few minutes during your day to learn and grow your mindset to help you lead a happy, peaceful life.

My healthy connections are:

_____

_____

_____

10. **Help others**

Most of us are gifted with a variety of resources in our life. We all have the ability to help others in various ways if we have the mind to help. Taking a few minutes during our day to help someone at home or someone outside your family can bring lots of happiness to our minds. When we start helping others, we will notice that we have so much to offer to the world to make it a beautiful place. When you help someone, do it genuinely and not to get something from the other person because then it will become transactional and will not bring any internal change within you.

What can you do to help someone within and outside your family?

_____

11. **Self-control**

When your mind asks you to jump from one activity to another, stop and don't listen. Ask yourself, should I carry this out or can this wait? You are the captain of the ship, so be the master instead of being the slave and listening to everything that your mind tells you. Once you develop this habit, you will notice that you are better able to manage your mind with the steering in your control.

12. **Silence**

Practice staying in silence for at least 5 minutes every day. It is a very powerful practice to develop internal mental strength. When we are silent, we will be able to listen to the chattering of our mind and know what is happening within us. However, if we have no time for the crying baby within us it will remain unattended and create more trouble.

13. **Acceptance**

Accept people and situations as they are without bringing in your expectations.

14. **Let go and forgive**

Let go of situations and people who are not in your control. Things that you need to let go of are the past, future, and people who you cannot control. Forgive within your mind the events or people who have caused you shame, guilt, and suffering.

15. **Detachment**

Be like a tree or a river that gives without any expectations. You are also part of the planet and are created for a purpose.

Live your purpose by serving others and helping them. Stay detached to the results of your actions and in your interactions with people around you.

16. **Positive self-talk**

We create the stories that we run in our own minds. The self-talk that we replay in our minds is mostly based on our own imaginations and memories from our past. These thoughts are highly unlikely to be real. Instead of criticizing ourselves with negative self-talk, we all have the ability to regulate our thoughts to positivity and transform our own thinking. As we continue this pattern, we will be able to catch the culprit of negative self-talk and redirect the energy positively to work in our favor.

By developing and inculcating these powerful practices into our daily life, we can develop a mental hygiene that develops our internal environment and prevents the external environment from affecting us. When we create such a peaceful internal environment that is made of strong walls of self-control, focus, detachment, courage, willpower, determination, perseverance, and devotion, nothing in this world can shake us. Life becomes easy to live and enjoy with a strong mind that is unshaken by the storms of people or situations around us. It is this life that every one of us can recreate and relive making every day a celebration for yourself and for the people around you.

CHAPTER 20

UNSHAKEABLE WOMEN FROM ANCIENT WISDOM

❧ ❧

"Where women are worshiped, there the gods dwell."
- Manusmriti 3.55-59

SITA

Sita was a mythological character who lived and showcased the ideal character of a woman through the great epic *Ramayana*. According to the story of Ramayana, Sita was born and found as a baby on a farm by the King Janaka. Later, King Janaka brought her up with strong principles and values. Sita chose the most perfect prince as her life partner, Lord Sri Rama, who was the great avatar of Maha Vishnu. Soon after their marriage, Sri Rama was exiled to the forest, and Sita decided to accompany him, leaving behind her luxurious and royal life. In the forest, Sita went through hard times and was kidnapped by the King Ravana who abducted her out of revenge towards Prince Lakshmana. Sita was separated from Sri Rama and lived a life of loneliness, enduring physical and emotional pain for many months. Regardless of the hardships, Sita had complete faith that Sri Rama would somehow rescue her from her suffering. It was her complete surrender and faith that gave her the strength to endure her difficulty and adhere to her values. Sita remained patient and waited for Lord Rama relentlessly.

Sita also brought up her children successfully as a single mother who modeled courage and strength before her children.

When Sita was asked to prove her character in public through a fire test, she refused to follow the order and stood up for herself.

Sita represents a strong woman who rose above her emotional suffering through her values of patience, faith, endurance, courage, willpower, forgiveness, perseverance, and unconditional love.

AHALYA

Ahalya was an ancient mythological character depicted in the great epic *Ramayana*. She was well known for her beauty and was the wife of the great Gautama Rishi. Ahalya went through emotional suffering of guilt, shame, and rejection after her husband cursed her to be a stone for having fallen in the trap of Lord Indra, who disguised himself as Gautama Maharishi, and losing her fidelity. Although it was not Ahalya's fault, she was still blamed and cursed to be hidden from the whole world. Ahalya, who was helpless and stuck, performed intense penance, chanting the Rama mantra that is believed to free from emotional pain for many years. When Ahalya attained her mental purity, Lord Sri Rama appeared before her and freed her from all her sufferings.

Ahalya represents the characters of patience, devotion, and perseverance that led her to win the blessings of Lord Sri Rama.

KUNTI

Kunti was a princess who was born to King Pritha. After her birth, her father gave her to his brother Kuntibhoja as he did not have any children. Later, Kuntibhoja had other children, but Kunti was still his favorite because of her character. Kunti had received special powers from the great sage Durvasa as a gift for serving him while he was in the kingdom. The special powers were in the form of mantras that she could use to fulfill her desires. It is these mantras that became the reason for the birth of Karna and the mighty Pandavas who won the Mahabharata war. Kunti was married to the King Pandu but lost him at a very early age when her children were small. So she had to move to her husband's kingdom to take care of them while residing with her brother-in-law Dhritarashtra, Gandhari, and their entire family. Despite having to live in a challenging environment, she brought up her sons based on dharma and eventually turned them into the best warriors during that period. She stood with her sons throughout the difficult times and offered them the right guidance, advice, encouragement, and support that made them stand up to protect their kingdom and fight the war.

Kunti was an ardent devotee of Lord Krishna and is said to have prayed for him to give her all the grief in the world so that she would remember the Lord at all times. Kunti represents the strong character of virtuous women and the principles of perseverance, forgiveness, willpower, humility, and surrender. Even during the most challenging situations, she did not give up but remained strong, offering support and wisdom to protect the kingdom.

DRAUPADI

Draupadi was yet another strong mythological character who lived during the time of the Mahabharata war. Draupadi was believed to have been born from a Yagna conducted by the King Drupada.

She later married the great Prince Arjuna during the Swayamvara organized by her father, King Drupada.

Draupadi went through severe humiliation when the Pandavas lost the dice game and were asked to offer all their wealth, including Draupadi. Draupadi, who was innocent, was dragged by her hair before Duryodhana to quench his revenge towards the Pandavas. Helpless, Draupadi reached out for support to everyone around her. However, everyone in the palace including the Pandavas sat with their heads down without taking the slightest effort to stop her from having to go through humiliation. When she realized that nobody around her could rescue her from humiliation, she prayed and surrendered to God in the form of Lord Krishna for help. The power of her surrender made the length of her robe increase so that Dushasana became tired of pulling her robe and failed to disrobe her.

Draupadi represents a woman of kindness, courage, intelligence, wisdom, devotion, forgiveness, willpower, and perseverance.

There have been many such strong ancient women who rose above their emotional suffering and led a marvelous life even during the most uncertain periods of their life. In spite of the numerous humiliations, abduction, and severe losses, they did not break down. They did not run away or end their life in weakness but instead proved their true worth before the world that has made us still remember their names and stories even today.

Life is a blessing given to you. Weep not when a challenging situation or person comes before you. Realize your true power, and stand up for yourself courageously. You don't need the whole world by your side to live your life to your fullest. You just need a powerful mind, and the rest will follow.

CONCLUSION

"Pain is inevitable, suffering is optional."
- Buddha

PAIN DOES NOT HAVE THE power to steal your peace unless you allow it. You have only one chance to live in this beautiful world. To make it painful or peaceful resides in your hands. So don't let any pain in your life stop you from living a happy and peaceful life. It is your birthright to live a life of peace. Let not the challenges or people around you snatch it away from you. Rise above your pain, conquer your mind, and recreate your future. Without peace in our hearts, we cannot bring peace in the world. As Mahatma Gandhi said, "Be the change that you wish to see in this world." Consistently working on your mind can shift the gray clouds of ignorance away and bring in the light of peace and wisdom into your life. We spend most of our time in this life with our own minds. If your mind is not happy you cannot be happy nor can you make anyone else in this world happy.

Peace is in simple living, harmony in what we think, say, and act, doing our duty with sincerity, and not causing harm through our thoughts, words, or actions to other fellow beings. What you sow is what you reap.

There is no better companion in this world than a mind that is peaceful.

If you have won the mind, you have won the world.

We become true humans only when we release ourselves from the lower levels of our mind by developing positive virtues of love, kindness, and compassion that serve us and others. Only if you are human can you become divine. May the universe give you the ability to develop an inner world filled with peace that fills the outer world with peace.

I hope you found the wisdom shared in this book valuable in your life. I would love to hear your thoughts and feedback. Please email me at samsarga.ca@gmail.com to send your questions or comments on this book.

Bibliography

Bhagavad Gita. Vintage, 2000.

Brahma. "Brahma Lekh | Progressive Indian Articles," n.d. https://brah. ma/lekh/.

Brewer, Judson. *Unwinding Anxiety: New Science Shows How to Break the Cycles of Worry and Fear to Heal Your Mind*. Penguin, 2022.

Brown, Brené. *Atlas of the Heart: Mapping Meaningful Connection and the Language of Human Experience*. Random House, 2021.

Burgin, Timothy. "Yoga Basics: Yoga Poses, Meditation, History, Yoga Philosophy & More." *Yoga Basics*, June 11, 2020. https://www. yogabasics.com/.

Chinmayananda, Swami. *A MANUAL OF SELF UNFOLDMENT*. Central Chinmaya Mission Trust, 2007.

Chinmayananda, Swami. *THE ART OF MAN MAKING PART I*. Central Chinmaya Mission Trust, 2015.

"Commentary on the Mundaka Upanishad - Chapter 1: Section 2," n.d. https://www.swami-krishnananda.org/mundak1/mundak1_2.html.

Dagny. "Diseases and Associated Chakras." *Reiki Rays*, April 27, 2021. https://reikirays.com/18039/diseases-and-associated-chakras/.

Deccan Herald. "News: Latest & Breaking News, Latest News Headlines | Deccan Herald," n.d. https://www.deccanherald.com/.

Dolls of India. "Dolls of India - Indian Paintings, Sculptures, Jewelry, Apparel, Books," n.d. https://www.dollsofindia.com/.

"Energy Zone Chart | Spinning®," n.d. https://spinning.com/energy-zone-chart/. "Main Home," n.d. https://vedantavision.org/.

Dr Travis Bradberry & Dr Jean Greaves. *Emotional Intelligence 2.0.* Perseus Books Group, 2009

Forbes. "Forbes," n.d. https://www.forbes.com/.

Fran. "World Mental Health Day | The State of Global Mental Health - FutureLearn." FutureLearn, December 6, 2021. https://www.futurelearn.com/info/blog/world-mental-health-day.

"Google Sites: Sign-In," n.d. https://sites.google.com/site/swamiramateachings/swami-rama-digging-treasure.

Gusev, Marjan, J.F. Tasic, Darja Rudan Tasic, Shushma Patel, Dilip Patel, and Biljana Veselinovska. "MindGym - IPTV for Elderly People." In *Springer EBooks*, 155–64, 2014. https://doi.org/10.1007/978-3-319-11564-1_16.

Hawkins, David R., MD PhD. *The Map of Consciousness Explained: A Proven Energy Scale to Actualize Your Ultimate Potential.* Hay House, Inc, 2020.

Harris,Russ. *"The Confidence Gap,"* Trumpeter ,Sep 13, 2011 Forbes. "Forbes," n.d. https://www.forbes.com/.

"Health News - Medical News Today," n.d. https://www.medicalnewstoday.com/.

"Hindu Women as Life Partner," n.d. https://www.esamskriti.com/e/Culture/Indian-Culture/Hindu-women-as-life-partner-1.aspx.

"ISTA - Internet Sacred Text Archive Home," n.d. https://www.sacred-texts.com/.

Jha, Shuvi. "Vedic Teachings about Womanhood - Hindu American Foundation." Hindu American Foundation, December 6, 2019. https://www.hinduamerican.org/blog/vedic-teachings-about-womanhood-2/.

Kabat-Zinn, Jon. *Full Catastrophe Living: Using the Wisdom of Your Body and Mind to Face Stress, Pain, and Illness*, 2008. http://ci.nii.ac.jp/ncid/BB19776576.

Live and Dare. "Live and Dare: Meditation, Self-Discipline, and Spirituality," September 1, 2022. https://liveanddare.com/.

"National Center for Biotechnology Information," n.d. https://www.ncbi.nlm.nih.gov/.

Lonely Philosopher. "Lonely Philosopher," June 16, 2022. https://www.lonelyphilosopher.com/.

Mcleod, Saul, PhD. "Maslow's Hierarchy of Needs." *Simply Psychology*, July 12, 2023. https://www.simplypsychology.org/maslow.html.

Melissa. "Online Yoga Classes and Programs - Ekhart Yoga." Ekhart Yoga, July 19, 2023. https://www.ekhartyoga.com/.

Musicians' Health Collective. "Musicians' Health Collective," n.d. http://www.musicianshealthcollective.com/.

Pasricha, Neil. *The Happiness Equation: Want Nothing + Do Anything = Have Everything*. Random House, 2017.

Pioneer. "English News Paper | Breaking News | Latest Today News in English | News Headlines India - The Pioneer." The Pioneer, n.d. https://www.dailypioneer.com/.

"Practical Sanskrit," n.d. https://blog.practicalsanskrit.com/.

Psych Central. "Psych Central - Trusted Mental Health, Depression, Bipolar, ADHD and Psychology," n.d. https://psychcentral.com/. "Home," n.d. https://erikabelanger.com/.

Reinhardt, Kassandra. "Yoga Journal | Yoga Poses - Sequences - Philosophy - Events." Yoga Journal, July 25, 2023. https://www.yogajournal.com/.

"Sanskrit Verses: Third Mundaka - The Mundaka Upanishad - Sanskrit Verses," n.d. https://www.swami-krishnananda.org/mundak/mun_sanb.html.

"ScienceDirect.Com | Science, Health and Medical Journals, Full Text Articles and Books.," n.d. https://www.sciencedirect.com/.

Srivastava, Sonal. "What is Dukkha." SpeakingTree, October 18, 2013. https://www.speakingtree.in/blog/what-is-dukkha.

Stokes, Victoria. "Root Chakra Healing: Techniques to Activate, Unblock, and Balance." Healthline, October 25, 2021.

https://www.healthline.com/health/mind-body/root-chakra-healing#what-is-it.

Stories From All Around the World! "Muddy Water (Wisdom, Buddhism)," January 31, 2015. https://mythologystories.wordpress.com/2015/01/31/muddy-water/.

"Stress Canada," n.d. https://stresscanada.org/.

The New Indian Express. "The Pain of Existence..." *The New Indian Express*, May 16, 2012. https://www.newindianexpress.com/states/karnataka/2010/dec/07/the-pain-of-existence-209066.html.

V, Jayaram. "Hinduwebsite.Com - The Real Hindu Website," n.d. https://www.hinduwebsite.com/.

"Vasanas," n.d. https://www.sivanandaonline.org/?cmd=displayrightsection§ion_id=1746&parent=1239&format=html.

Vivekananda, Swami. *Patanjali's Yoga Sutras*. Prabhat Prakashan, 2022.

Vivekananda, Swami. *Thoughts on the Gita*. Advaita Ashrama (A Publication House of Ramakrishna Math, Belur Math), 1963.

VivekaVani. "Swami Vivekananda Quotes - VivekaVani," June 27, 2023. https://vivekavani.com/.

We Are Rethink Mental Illness. "No Matter How Bad Things Are, We Can Help.," n.d. https://www.rethink.org/.

Woods, Lauren. *Emotionfull: A Guide to Self-Care for Your Mental Health and Emotions*, 2020.

Yes Vedanta. "Knowledge of the Seers," May 20, 2023. https://www.yesvedanta.com/.

"Yoga International: Study And Download Yoga Online," n.d. https://yogainternational.com/.

Acknowledgments

Thanks to all my spiritual Gurus, mentors, coaches, and teachers who have inspired, guided, and taught me valuable lessons to change my life and the life of others around me. Thanks to all my special clients who allowed me to share their stories in this book to help more readers.

Thanks to my book coach, Karen Pina, and editor, Sarah Fraps, for going through each chapter in detail and providing me with your valuable feedback and support that helped me to make my dream come true.

Author Bio

Amritha is a Jay Shetty Certified Life and Success Coach who specializes in Emotional Wellness and Transformation Coaching.

Through her online school Samsarga, she offers coaching guidance, mentoring and support to empower women who have gone through toxic relationships and lost their true identity thereby helping them to rise above self-doubt and become self-reliant.

Her coaching services have been featured in online magazines—*New York Weekly*, *CEO Weekly*, *Influencer Daily*, *Kivo Daily*, and *Disrupt Magazine*.

Her school also offers online courses in Sanskrit, Reiki training, as well as Vocal and Veena classes.

She is the host of the talk show *The Peace Bridge* on VoiceAmerica, a mentor on Wisdom, a Usui-Certified Reiki Master, a speaker, Udemy Sanskrit instructor with over 10,000 students across 142 countries, a blogger on Medium and Core Spirit, and an Indian classical musician.

URGENT PLEA!
Thank You For Reading My Book!
I really appreciate all of your feedback and
I love hearing what you have to say.
I need your input to make the next version of this
book, and my future books, better.

Please take 2 minutes now to leave a helpful review on
Amazon letting me know what you thought of the book:
www.samsarga.ca/review
Thanks so much!
- Amritha Kailas

Manufactured by Amazon.ca
Bolton, ON